AF782519

CRIMINAL JUSTICE

IN TEXAS

THIRD EDITION

MICHAEL KANE
Coastal Bend Community College
Beeville, Texas

PEARSON
Prentice Hall

Upper Saddle River, New Jersey 07458

Executive Editor: Frank Mortimer, Jr.
Assistant Editor: Sara Holle
Production Editor: Barbara Cappuccio
Director of Manufacturing and Production: Bruce Johnson
Managing Editor: Mary Carnis
Manufacturing Buyer: Cathleen Petersen
Creative Director: Cheryl Asherman
Cover Design Coordinator: Miguel Ortiz
Cover Design: Denise Brown
Cover Image: Day Williams/Photo Researchers, Inc.

Pearson Education LTD.
Pearson Education Singapore, Pte. Ltd
Pearson Education, Canada, Ltd
Pearson Education–Japan
Pearson Education Australia PTY, Limited
Pearson Education North Asia Ltd
Pearson Educaçion de Mexico, S.A. de C.V.
Pearson Education Malaysia, Pte. Ltd

PEARSON
Prentice Hall

10 9 8 7 6 5 4 3 2 1
ISBN 0-13-114034-5

TABLE OF CONTENTS

PREFACE

Criminal Justice in Texas is an introductory look at the practical application of criminal justice in Texas. The text will allow students to study the uniqueness and the breadth of the Texas criminal justice system. Students will be exposed to the services of protection and the administration of justice the State of Texas provides to its residents and its visitors.

This text showcases many contemporary issues in the Texas criminal justice system. The supplement used online research and web sites of many Texas criminal justice agencies. Because on-line criminal justice databases were used, students have the most recent information about the Texas criminal justice system that is possible to print.

Criminal Justice in Texas is comprehensive and interesting, addressing all major elements of the criminal justice system in Texas. It examines crime and the law in Texas, law enforcement throughout the state, the Texas judicial system, corrections in Texas, the juvenile justice system, and the drug problem in Texas.

Finally,the text encourages student research via the Internet by providing an extensive list of World Wide Web links to information on criminal justice in Texas. Texas, with its many technology-related industries, is a worldwide leader in the electronic information age. This leadership has provided an avenue for a vast majority of criminal justice agencies in Texas to publish and maintain their own web page on the Internet.

Throughout the text, you will find quotations which have been taken verbatim from legal documents, such as the Texas Penal Code and the Constitution. Any misspellings or other irregularities are reproduced exactly as they appear in the original documents.

CHAPTER 1

THE STATE OF TEXAS

INTRODUCTION

Texas is located in the west south central region of the United States. It borders the Gulf of Mexico on the southeast, Mexico on the southwest, New Mexico on the west, Louisiana on the east, and Oklahoma and Arkansas on the north and northeast. The capital city of Texas is Austin. The state motto is "Friendship," the state bird is the mockingbird, the state flower is the bluebonnet, and the state tree is the pecan. Texas' nickname is the "Lone Star State."

THE HISTORY OF TEXAS

Early Texas

Texas was originally inhabited by a variety of Native American tribes, many of which lived in agricultural settlements. Different regions of Texas were home to different tribes. In eastern Texas, the natives were organized into two confederacies, the Hasinai and the Caddo. The Spanish explorers first arriving in eastern Texas met the Hasinai and took their word for allies, "techas," to mean both the area and the people living there. South Texas was home to the Coahuiltecan Indians while the Apache lived in the western part of the state.

Spanish Exploration of Texas

The first Europeans to visit Texas were the Spanish, who sent a number of expeditions to the region. Some were explorers, while others were searching for gold and other treasures. The first Spanish explorers, led by Alonso Alvarez de Pineda, arrived in Texas in about 1519 while mapping the coast of the Gulf of Mexico. The Spanish also built the first Franciscan missions in Texas in 1682, near what is now El Paso.

The French developed an interest in Texas as well. In 1685, Rene-Robert Cavelier, Sieur de La Salle, established a colony known as Fort Saint Louis. However, the colony was struck by disease and was destroyed by Indians shortly before a Spanish expedition, which also planned to destroy the settlement, arrived. A second attempt at French settlement occurred in 1714, when a French trading expedition founded a settlement on the Rio Grande.

During the late 17th and early 18th centuries, Spain continued to send expeditions into Texas, and established missions and forts throughout the region. One of the main reasons for the Spanish development of the mission system in eastern Texas was to prevent further French settlement in what the Spanish considered to be their territory. In 1718, near what is now San Antonio, a fort known as San Antonio de Bexar was built to guard the mission of San Antonio de Valero. The mission was later called the Alamo. San Antonio became the seat of Spanish government in Texas in 1772.

Spanish influence over Texas became severely weakened between 1800 and 1820. There were several attempts during this period to set up independent governments in Texas. Most of these were made by Mexicans who desired freedom from Spain. They often received assistance from Americans. In 1821, when Mexico obtained independence from Spain, it claimed Texas as part of the Empire of Mexico and in 1824, Mexico became a republic.

In 1820, Spanish officials in Mexico granted permission for an American, Moses Austin, to establish an American colony in Texas. Although Austin died shortly after submitting his request to Mexico, his son, Stephen Fuller Austin, was allowed to continue the project after Mexico gained independence from Spain. He brought 300 families to Texas, officially establishing a settlement in southeast Texas in 1822. Mexico also gave land grants to other Americans, allowing them to establish colonies in Texas. These contractors, who were known as *empresarios*, founded a number of colonies during the 1820s.

However, problems between Mexico and the American settlers quickly developed. The new settlers spoke only English, refused to assimilate into Mexican culture, and advocated slavery, a practice to which the Mexicans were opposed. Many of the Anglo-American settlers wanted to become independent from Mexico. This led to the 1826 Fredonian Rebellion, an attempt to create an independent Republic of Fredonia. Shortly after this attempt failed, the Mexican government realized that there were more Anglo-Americans than Mexicans living in Texas. By 1830, concern about the increasing number of Americans settling in Texas led Mexico to restrict American immigration into Texas and to prohibit the importation of slaves into the area.

Texas Becomes an Independent Republic

In 1834, General Antonio Lopez de Santa Anna, a Mexican soldier and politician, overthrew the constitutional government of Mexico and proclaimed himself dictator. His poor treatment of the American settlers led them to revolt against Mexico in an action known as the Texas Revolution. The first battle of the Revolution occurred in October, 1835. On December 11, 1835, the colonists captured San Antonio. General Santa Anna marched on the city and attacked the colonists, who retreated into the Alamo. Attacks on the former mission continued until March 6, 1836, when the Alamo fell. During the siege on the Alamo, American Texan rebel leaders declared independence from Mexico and selected Sam Houston as the commander of the rebel army and David G. Burnet as temporary president. They also adopted a constitution that protected their right to slavery, an institution that had been abolished by Mexican law. For the next month, Santa Anna forced the rebels to retreat. However, on April 21, 1836, in the Battle of San Jacinto, Sam Houston's army made a surprise attack on the Mexican forces. During this battle, Santa Anna's force of 1,600 soldiers was killed or captured by Houston's 800-man army. Only nine Texans died during this battle. Santa Anna was captured, and the war was ended. Santa Anna was forced to recognized Texas' independence and to retreat south of the Rio Grande.

The region became known as the Republic of Texas. The first election was held in September, 1836. Sam Houston was elected president, and the new republic voted to join the United States. However, although the South wanted Texas to become a state, the North opposed admission because slavery was allowed in Texas. As a result, Texas remained an independent republic for almost ten years.

As more American and European settlers arrived in Texas, the Native Americans were rapidly being forced out of the region. Sam Houston had negotiated a treaty with the Cherokee Indians during the Texas Revolution, reserving for the Cherokee certain lands in eastern Texas. However, the new republic refused to keep the treaty, leading to hostilities between the Cherokee and white settlers. Eventually, the Cherokee were defeated at the Battle of the Neches in 1839, and were forced north into what is now Oklahoma.

Texas in the 19th Century

On December 29, 1845, Texas became the 28th state in the United States. Mexico immediately ended diplomatic relationships with the United States and arguments developed over the location of the Mexico-Texas boundary. In 1846, Congress declared war on Mexico. The Mexican War lasted two years, ending in 1848 with the signing of the Treaty of Guadalupe Hidalgo. Under this treaty, Mexico renounced all claims to Texas, and the United States obtained additional land in the southwest that would later become California, Nevada, Utah, and parts of Colorado, Arizona, New Mexico, and Wyoming. The United States agreed to pay $15 million to Mexico and to settle all legal claims outstanding against Mexico.

During the 1850s, Texas was a very attractive destination for settlers, with the northeast region and the area east of Waco and Fort Worth becoming the most popular areas. A total of 89 new counties were organized during this time.

In February 1861, Texas seceded from the United States, despite strong Union feeling in some areas of the state. Governor Sam Houston was removed from office after refusing to take an oath to support the constitution of the Confederate States of America. Texas joined the Confederacy in March and fought for the South during the Civil War. Although General Robert E. Lee surrendered on April 9, 1865, this news did not reach Texas, and the last battle of the Civil War was fought at Palmito Hill, Texas on May 13, 1865. Similarly, blacks in Texas did not hear about the 1863 Emancipation Proclamation until June 19, 1865 when the Union Army arrived in Galveston.

During the Reconstructionist period, Texas was dominated by a group known as the Radicals, who sympathized with the North. The Ku Klux Klan rose to power in the state during this period. Texas was readmitted to the Union in 1870, after ratifying the 13th, 14th, and 15th Amendments to the United States Constitution. The 13th Amendment abolished slavery and the 15th Amendment gave blacks the right to vote. The 14th Amendment essentially applied the Bill of Rights to the states and gave the federal government the authority to enforce state violations of individual rights. Ratification of these three amendments was a requirement for readmission for those states who had seceded from the Union.

The population of Texas increased significantly after the Civil War; between 1870 and 1900 the state moved from the 19th most populous state to the 6th most populous state in the country. Cattle drives became an important part of the Texas economy. By the 1880s, the construction of railroads across the state ended the cattle drives but significantly assisted new settlers in reaching the western portions of the state. Settlers in this region were protected from bandits and hostile Indians by the Texas Rangers, which had been organized in 1835. The railroads also increased the influence of cotton on the state's economy by allowing the crop to be shipped to Houston or St. Louis for international trade. By 1890, the state produced over one-third of all cotton grown in the country.

By the end of the 19th century, discrimination against blacks and Mexicans was becoming increasingly common. After the 1896 U.S. Supreme Court case of *Plessey v. Ferguson*[1], Texas passed "Jim Crow" laws segregating public facilities, residential neighborhoods, and transportation. Black voters were disenfranchised, first through violence and then through the development of all-white primaries, and finally through the approval of a poll tax. Mexicans in Texas were disenfranchised either because they were Mexican (rather than American) citizens or because of the white-only primaries and the poll tax.

Texas During the 20th Century

Texas began to develop oil and gas refineries in 1901. Agriculture also increased as grazing land was irrigated and converted to farmland. Urbanization increased significantly in Texas; the number of cities and towns doubled between 1900 and 1920.

Prior to World War I, a group of Democrats known as Progressives gained control of the party and advocated a number of social and economic reforms (although racial injustice was not one of their concerns). Reforms focused on state institutions, the enfranchisement of white women, and the passage of Prohibition. Progressive Democrats passed laws that created orphanages and state mental institutions. They also reformed the state's prison system, abolishing the convict lease system and segregating prison inmates by sex, race, age, and type of offense.

During World War I, a number of federal military training camps were located in Texas. In 1925, Miriam A. ("Ma") Ferguson was elected the first woman governor of the state, making Texas the second state in the United States (after Wyoming) to have a female governor, and the first to have a woman elected to the office. Ferguson's husband, James Ferguson, had previously served as governor of the state as well. Both were staunch opponents of the Ku Klux Klan and helped to reduce its political power in the state.

During World War II, military training camps were again located in Texas, with over 1.25 million troops receiving training in the state. After the war ended, Texas began to move from a rural economy based primarily on farming to an urban industrial economy. In the 1960s, Texas became significantly involved in the United States space program. In 1962, NASA constructed a Manned Spacecraft Center near Houston, which became the headquarters of the manned spacecraft program in 1964. It was renamed the Lyndon B. Johnson Space Center in 1973. The assassination of President John F. Kennedy in Dallas on November 22, 1963, also brought national attention to Texas.

The population of Texas increased significantly during the 1960s; by 1975, Texas had become the third largest state in the country by population. The state's economy focused on oil, defense, and agriculture. By 1970, much of east and west Texas was virtually uninhabited, consisting primarily of enormous farms.

During the 1970s and early 1980s, both population and economy were booming. After the 1973 OPEC oil embargo, the price of oil in Texas skyrocketed, resulting in an economic boom that led to a significant population increase. However, after the embargo ended in the early 1980s, rapid declines in the prices of natural gas and oil, along with a reduction in the increasingly large amounts of money spent on defense, greatly damaged the state's economy. The state sales tax was increased in an attempt to raise revenue. At this time, Texas was also under a court order to improve and modernize state prisons. In the early 1990s, the governor allocated more funds to improve prisons, as well as roads and bridges. However, this led to a decrease in the monies available for public and higher education. During the 1990s, Texas voters continued to oppose taxes and spending for public services.

Texas' economy began to improve in 1989, leading to renewed immigration into the state. By the early 1990s, the state's population had increased by 1.5 million. Many Mexicans immigrated to Texas, both legally and illegally, making Hispanics the state's largest minority group. The signing of NAFTA in 1994 has led to economic benefits for some parts of the state, particularly the Houston, Dallas-Fort Worth, and San Antonio triangle However, many border areas still have high unemployment.

On February 28, 1993, the U.S. Bureau of Alcohol, Tobacco, and Firearms (ATF) responded to accusations that a religious group in Waco, Texas, the Branch Davidians, had illegal weapons hidden in their compound. The ATF's raid on the Branch Davidian compound resulted in the death of four ATF agents and at least five Branch Davidian members, and led to a 51-day standoff between the FBI and the Branch Davidians. On April 19, federal agents attempted to force the Branch Davidians out of the compound by shooting tear gas into the buildings. A fire broke out and a large number of Branch Davidian members, including 25 children, remained in the buildings and died in the fire.

TEXAS TODAY

Texas is the second largest state in the country by land area (only Alaska has a larger land area) and comprises 7 percent of the land area of the United States. The state has a total area of 267,277 square miles, which includes 4,959 square miles of inland water and 404 square miles of coastal water over which the state has jurisdiction. The state runs 770 miles from east to west and 800 miles from north to south. The average elevation of the state is 1,700 feet above sea level.

According to the 2000 census, Texas is the second largest state by population, after California. The 2000 census reported a total population of 20,851,820, an increase of almost 23 percent over the 1990 figure. The average population density is 79.6 persons per square mile. The most populous city in Texas is Houston, with a population of 1,953,631 in 2000. Other large cities include Dallas, San Antonio, Austin, Fort Worth, and El Paso.[2]

In 2000, 71 percent of the state's population were white, 11.5 percent were black, and 2.7 percent Asian. The remainder of the population includes Native Americans, Pacific Islanders (including Native Hawaiians), those of mixed heritage, and those who did not report ethnicity to the Census Bureau. Approximately 32 percent of the population are reported as being of Hispanic origin, although they may be of any race. Most of the population lives in urban areas.[3]

Texas has a total of 254 counties, more than any other state in the United States. The state elects two United States Senators and 30 members of the House of Representatives, for a total of 32 electoral votes. The current state constitution was adopted in 1876.

NOTES

1. *Plessey v. Ferguson*, 163 U.S. 537 (1896)
2. U.S Census Bureau (http://www.census.gov)
3. *Ibid*

CHAPTER 2

INTRODUCTION TO TEXAS CRIMINAL LAW

THE STRUCTURE OF THE GOVERNMENT

Texas law is found in the State Constitution and in the Texas Penal Code. Both have been frequently modified, amended, and altered over the past century.

The current **Texas Constitution** was ratified in 1876.[1] It has been amended numerous times since then. Earlier constitutions were adopted in 1845, 1861, 1866, and 1869. The Texas Constitution is the primary law of the state, although it is subordinate to the United States Constitution. No criminal law or constitutional amendment enacted in Texas may conflict with or violate any individual rights which are guaranteed by the U.S. Constitution, the Bill of Rights, any other Constitutional Amendments, or any federal laws. If any part of the Texas Constitution or legal code is found to be in conflict with the U.S. Constitution or federal statutes, the Texas enactment is unconstitutional and must be changed.

The procedure for amending the Texas Constitution is discussed in Article 17, Section 1 of the Constitution. The new amendment must be proposed at either a regular or special session of the **Texas Legislature**. The proposal for submission must be approved by a two-thirds majority of the members of each of the two legislative houses. A brief statement explaining the nature of the proposed amendment must then be published at least twice in Texas newspapers and must be posted in the courthouse of each county. This statement must include the date of the election on the amendment and the exact wording of the proposition as it will appear on the election ballot. Finally, the proposal must then be approved by a majority of voters before it can become a part of the state constitution.

Like most states, Texas has three branches of government: executive, legislative, and judicial. This is specified in Article 2, Section 1 of the Texas Constitution, which also provides for separation of powers.

The Executive Branch

Article 4 of the Texas Constitution discusses Texas' **executive branch**, which consists of the following officers: Governor, Lieutenant Governor, Secretary of State, Comptroller of Public Accounts, Commissioner of the General Land Office, and Attorney General. Most of these officers are elected to four-year terms. Although some states limit the number of times the governor may be re-elected, in Texas the governor may serve an unlimited number of terms. The other officers, with the exception of the Secretary of State, are also elected by the voters and serve four-year terms as well. The Secretary of State is appointed by the governor with the advice and consent of the Senate and serves during the term of the governor.

To be elected to the office of governor or lieutenant governor of Texas, a candidate must be a citizen of the United States, at least 30 years of age, and a state resident for a minimum of five years immediately preceding election to office. The governor has the power to veto legislation that has been proposed by the state legislature. However, a two-thirds vote in both houses of the legislature may override the governor's veto.[2]

George W. Bush III, a Republican, was in his second term as governor when he was elected to the office of President of the United States. Bush resigned on December 21, 2000 and Lieutenant Governor Rick Perry was sworn in as the 47th governor of Texas. Perry served as governor for the remainder of Bush's term, and was elected to a four-year term on November 5, 2002.

The Legislative Branch

The **Legislature of the State of Texas** is discussed in Article III of the Texas Constitution and is the lawmaking branch of the government. The legislature is made up of two houses, a 31-member Senate and a 150-member House of Representatives. All members of the legislature are elected. Senators serve four-year terms while representatives serve two-year terms.

To serve as a member of the Texas Senate, a candidate must be a United States citizen, a qualified voter in the state, at least 26 years of age, a state resident for at least five years prior to the election, and a resident of the district from which he or she will be elected for at least one year immediately preceding the election. To serve as a member of the Texas House of Representatives, a candidate must be a United States citizen, a qualified voter, at least 21 years of age, a state resident for at least two years prior to the election, and a resident of the district from which he or she will be elected for at least one year immediately preceding the election.

Each house selects its own officers from among its membership. The presiding officer of the Senate is known as the **President Pro Tempore**. This officer also performs the duties of the Lieutenant Governor if that office becomes vacant for any reason. The presiding officer of the House of Representatives is known as the **Speaker of the House of Representatives**.

The Judicial Branch

The judicial branch of the government, which is discussed in Article V of the Texas Constitution, contains the various Texas courts. The court structure of Texas is somewhat more complicated than that of many other states. Texas has a five-level court structure, with two top-level appellate courts, an intermediate appellate court, state trial courts of general jurisdiction, county trial courts of limited jurisdiction, and local trial courts of limited jurisdiction.[3]

Unlike most states, Texas has two appellate courts of last resort. The **Texas Supreme Court** is made up of nine justices, one of whom serves as the chief justice. Supreme Court justices are elected to six-year terms. The Supreme Court has final appellate jurisdiction in all civil cases and all judicial cases but has no criminal jurisdiction.[4] The court with final appellate jurisdiction over criminal cases is known as the **Court of Criminal Appeals**. This court has nine judges, one of whom serves as the presiding judge. Judges are elected and serve six-year terms[5]. All cases involving a sentence of death are automatically appealed to the Court of Criminal Appeals from the trial court level.[6]

The state's intermediate appellate courts are known as **Courts of Appeals**. There is one Court of Appeals in each of the state's fourteen appellate districts. These courts have intermediate appellate jurisdiction in criminal and civil cases that have been appealed from district or county courts.[7]

The state is also divided into judicial districts, each of which has a **District Court** with one or more judges.[8] District courts are the state's trial courts of general jurisdiction and have original jurisdiction over all felony criminal cases, as well as civil cases involving at least $200, divorce cases, and various other matters.

Texas has several county-level courts which have limited jurisdiction. Each county is required by the Texas Constitution to have one **Constitutional County Court.**[9] The county judge, the presiding officer of the county court, is elected and serves a four-year term. County courts have limited criminal and civil jurisdiction and in some counties have appellate jurisdiction over cases appealed from justices of the peace or municipal courts. Because the Constitution specifically limits each county to only one constitutional county court, larger counties may also have **County Courts at Law** to assist the county court. The jurisdiction of county courts at law varies by county. In those counties that have them, the county courts at law (not the county court) have appellate jurisdiction over cases appealed from a justice of the peace or municipal court. Finally, some jurisdictions also have **Statutory Probate Courts** which have original jurisdiction over probate matters, guardianship issues, and mental health commitments. In some counties, specialized probate courts hear only probate matters.

Finally, the state has several local trial courts which also have limited jurisdiction. Each of the incorporated cities and towns in Texas has one or more **Municipal Courts**. Municipal courts have original jurisdiction over violations of city ordinances. In addition, each county in the state is divided into justice of the peace precincts. The number of precincts in a county (between one and eight) is determined by the county population. Each precinct has either one or two **Justice of the Peace Courts**, depending on the precinct population. These have original jurisdiction over minor civil cases as well as certain misdemeanor criminal cases, and also serve as small claims courts. The Texas court system is discussed in more detail in Chapter 5.

Passing a Law in Texas

In Texas, a bill may be introduced into either the House or the Senate and, after it has been passed by one of the two legislative houses, it may still be amended by the other. Each bill must first be referred to a committee which reports upon it prior to voting. The bill then goes to a floor vote in the originating house. After it is passed by this house, it is sent to the other house for review, where it may be passed, amended, altered, or rejected. If a bill is considered and defeated by either house, no other bill which contains the same substance may be passed into law during the same legislative session. If the bill passes both houses of the Texas Legislature, it is sent to the governor for approval; he/she may choose either to veto the bill or to sign it into law. The governor has ten days (not counting Sundays) to veto the bill. If the governor approves and signs the bill, or if he or she fails to veto it within ten days, the bill will become law. The legislature may, by a two-thirds vote of each house, enact a bill into law over the governor's veto.

THE TEXAS PENAL CODE

There are several sources of criminal law in Texas. These include:

- Federal and state constitutions
- Substantive criminal law
- Case law

Together, the Texas Constitution and the U.S. Constitution provide the basic framework for criminal law, first by focusing on individual rights and on the limitations placed on government power, and second by requiring the establishment of a judicial system. However, neither the federal nor the state constitution significantly emphasizes the creation or definition of crimes.

The primary source of **substantive criminal law** in Texas is the **Texas Penal Code**, which is part of the Texas Statutes.[10] The modern Texas Penal Code was first enacted in 1973. However, other statutes also contain laws which relate to crime and punishment. For example, The Texas Code of Criminal Procedure contains laws relating to procedures such as arrests, trials, and sentencing. Other statutes that define criminal actions include the Family Code, the Transportation Code, the Alcohol Beverage Code, the Agriculture Code, the Business and Commerce Code, the Tax Code, the Education Code, and the Health and Safety Code, among others.

Statutory citations from the Texas Penal Code resemble case citations. A sample statutory citation is **Pen §19.01**. Pen is the abbreviation for the Texas Penal Code and 19.01 refers to the specific section number of the statute. This particular statute lists the types of criminal homicide in Texas.

The Texas Penal Code was originally based on the English common law, which became the law of the original thirteen colonies and then evolved into the law of the individual states as they entered the union. However, the current Texas legal system is based entirely on written law, so that all crimes are codified. Pen §1.03(a) states that:

> Conduct does not constitute an offense unless it is defined as an offense by statute, municipal ordinance, order of a county commissioners court, or rule authorized by and lawfully adopted under a statute.

Basically, unless a certain behavior or act has been specifically defined as an offense, it is not a crime under the law in Texas.

Case law consists of appellate court decisions or opinions which interpret the meaning of the law. Essentially, case law is made by judges when they hand down decisions in court. Because of the principle of ***stare decisis***, or precedent, a decision made by a judge in one court will be followed by later judges in the state until the same court reverses its decision or until the decision is overturned by a higher court.

The Texas Penal Code contains two types of law, substantive and procedural. **Substantive criminal law** includes definitions of specific crimes and identifies the punishments associated with each criminal act. Chapter 19 of the Penal Code, which discusses the topic of criminal homicide, is an example of substantive criminal law. **Procedural law**, on the other hand, focuses on the methods that are used to enforce the substantive criminal law. In other words, procedural law outlines the rules that the state must follow when dealing with crimes and criminals. These include the procedures that must be used to investigate crimes, arrest suspects, and carry out formal prosecution. The protection against double jeopardy is an example of procedural law.

THE DEFINITION AND CLASSIFICATION OF CRIME

In Texas, according to Pen §12.02, "offenses are designated as felonies or misdemeanors." In Texas, the difference between the two types of crimes is not determined by the offense itself, or by the action committed by the offender, but by the possible punishment or by the designation of the crime as a felony or a misdemeanor by the Penal Code.

Felonies are the most serious offenses in Texas. Pen §1.07(a)(23) defines a felony as "an offense so designated by law or punishable by death or confinement in a penitentiary." A **misdemeanor** is defined in Pen §1.07(a)(31) as "an offense so designated by law or punishable by fine, by confinement in jail, or by both fine and confinement in jail." Based on these definitions, even if the Penal Code does not specifically identify a crime as a misdemeanor or a felony, the classification can easily be inferred from the prescribed sentence.

Felonies are classified into five categories, based on the relative seriousness of the crime. The five categories are listed in Pen §12.04 and the associated punishments are outlined in Pen §12.31 through Pen §12.35.

- A **capital felony** is the most serious category of crime in Texas. It is punishable either by death or by life imprisonment in a state penal institution. The only death penalty offense that has ever existed in Texas is the crime of capital murder. In a capital case, the state is required to state prior to trial whether or not they plan to seek the death penalty as punishment for the crime; this information must also be provided to prospective jury members.

- A **felony of the first degree** is punishable by imprisonment in a state prison for life, or by a term of imprisonment of not more than 99 years nor less than five years. The key difference between a life sentence and a sentence of 99 years is that a life sentence may not be discharged. Murder, other than capital murder, is a first degree felony in Texas. Aggravated robbery and aggravated sexual assault are other examples of first degree felonies. There are over 30 first degree felonies identified in the Texas Penal Law.

- A **felony of the second degree** is punishable by a term of imprisonment in a state prison for not more than 20 years or less than two years. There are approximately 45 second degree felonies listed in the Texas Statutes, particularly in the Penal Code and the Health and Safety Code. Examples include manslaughter, sexual assault, aggravated assault, and arson.

- A **felony of the third degree** is punishable by imprisonment in a state prison for a term of not more than ten years nor less than two years. Aggravated promotion of prostitution and aggravated perjury are examples of third degree felonies. There are approximately 75 third degree felony crimes in Texas.

- A **state jail felony** is the lowest category of felony offense in Texas. In most cases, a state jail felony is punishable by confinement in a state jail facility (as opposed to a state prison) for a term of not more than two years nor less than 180 days. Credit card and debit card abuse are examples of state jail felonies.

In addition to the terms of imprisonment mandated by statute for each of the above felony categories, the judge may also sentence the offender to pay a fine of not more than $10,000. This fine would be in addition to (not in lieu of) the sentence of incarceration.

Misdemeanors are also classified by degree, and may be categorized as Class A, Class B, or Class C. If a statute defines a crime as a misdemeanor but does not specify the degree, it is considered to be a Class C misdemeanor.[11] The penalties associated with misdemeanors are outlined in Pen §12.21 through Pen §12.23.

- A **Class A misdemeanor** is the most serious category of misdemeanors in Texas. Class A misdemeanors are punishable by either a fine of up to $4,000 or a term of imprisonment in a county jail for no more than one year, or by both the fine and term of imprisonment. Examples of Class A misdemeanors include simple assault, public lewdness, and the burglary of a coin-operated machine. Since 1974, Texas has steadily increased the maximum fine for these crimes. Between 1974 and 1991, the maximum fine for a Class A misdemeanor was $2,000. It was increased to $3,000 in 1991 and to the present level of $4,000 in 1994.

- A **Class B misdemeanor** is punishable by either a fine of no more than $2,000 or a jail term of no more than 180 days, or by both the fine and jail term. Prior to 1991, the maximum fine was $1,000; it was increased to $1,500 in 1991 and to $2,000 in 1994. Indecent exposure is an example of a Class B misdemeanor.

- Finally, a **Class C misdemeanor** is punishable by a fine of no more than $500. There is no term of imprisonment associated with Class C misdemeanor offenses. There are approximately 30 different Class C offenses *(not counting municipal ordinance violations and traffic tickets)* listed in the Penal Code, Transportation Code, and Health and Safety Code.

Texas also recognizes a number of **inchoate offenses**, which are essentially preparatory offenses that either attempt or lead to the commission of another crime. Preparatory offenses are discussed in Chapter 15 of the Penal Code and include **criminal attempt,**[12] **criminal conspiracy,**[13] and ***criminal solicitation.***[14]

The Criminal Act (*Actus Reus*) and Intent (*Mens Rea*)

All crimes have several general features or elements. One of these is ***actus reus***, or the **criminal act**. In Texas, the act or omission that constitutes a crime must be voluntary. According to Pen §6.01,

> (a) A person commits an offense only if he voluntarily engages in conduct, including an act, an omission, or possession.
> (b) Possession is a voluntary act if the possessor knowingly obtains or receives the thing possessed or is aware of his control of the thing for a sufficient time to permit him to terminate his control.
> (c) A person who omits to perform an act does not commit an offense unless a law ... provides that the omission is an offense or otherwise provides that he has a duty to perform the act.

Most criminal acts are deliberate and voluntary on the part of the offender. However, the specific act necessary to make up a crime will vary with each crime. Verbal actions (words) can be a sufficient action in, for example, the crime of perjury. Merely possessing something may be a sufficient act if the crime is one that involves illegal possession of goods, such as the possession of illegal drugs.

It is clear from Pen §6.01 that the criminal act may also consist of some form of omission or failure to act. An **omission** occurs when someone who has a legal duty to act fails to perform an action that is required by law. For example, a security guard who deliberately looks the other way while company property is stolen is a passive participant and is guilty of omission to act. Similarly, a parent or other legal caretaker who fails to adequately feed and shelter an infant has committed a crime by his or her failure to act.

Failing to act is only a crime of omission when an individual has a legal duty to act in that situation. For example, consider the case of a swimmer at a local public pool who develops a cramp while in deep water. The lifeguard on duty at the pool has a legal duty to act and, if s/he fails to go to the swimmer's assistance, would be guilty of a crime of omission. However, the other swimmers in the pool have only a moral duty to aid the distressed swimmer and if they fail to provide assistance would not be guilty of any crime. In addition, the omission or failure to act must also be voluntary for this statute to apply.

Another element of a crime is that of ***mens rea***, or the **guilty mind**. Pen §6.02 states that:

> (a) Except as provided in Subsection (b), a person does not commit an offense unless he intentionally, knowingly, recklessly, or with criminal negligence engages in conduct as the definition of the offense requires.
> (b) If the definition of an offense does not prescribe a culpable mental state, a culpable mental state is nevertheless required unless the definition plainly dispenses with any mental element.
> (c) If the definition of an offense does not prescribe a culpable mental state, but one is nevertheless required under Subsection (b), intent, knowledge, or recklessness suffices to establish criminal responsibility.
> (d) Culpable mental states are classified according to relative degrees, from highest to lowest, as follows:
> (1) intentional;
> (2) knowing;
> (3) reckless;
> (4) criminal negligence.
> (e) Proof of a higher degree of culpability than that charged constitutes proof of the culpability charged.

Thus, even if the individual has acted voluntarily, as discussed in Pen §6.01, the act generally is not a crime unless one of the four types of **culpable mental states** exist. The four culpable mental states are specifically defined in Pen §6.03:

- A crime is committed **intentionally** when the offender consciously desires to engage in the conduct or cause the outcome. The offender does not have to deliberately declare intent to be convicted of a crime. The intent may be inferred by the actions of the offender.

- A crime is committed **knowingly** when the offender is aware that his or her conduct violates the law and/or is aware that his or her conduct will cause a certain result.

- A crime is committed **recklessly** when the offender is aware of the risk of his/her actions and consciously disregards that risk. The risk must be substantial and unjustified and disregarding it must be a significant deviation from the behavior of a reasonable person.

- A crime is committed with **criminal negligence** when the offender fails to perceive a risk that would be perceived by any reasonable person. The key difference between recklessness and criminal negligence is that, to be negligent, the offender does not have to consciously be aware of the risk involved by his or her behavior.

There are some situations in which a culpable mental state is not required for an act to be a crime. These crimes are known as **strict liability offenses** and include crimes such as speeding and driving while intoxicated.

DEFENSES TO A CRIMINAL CHARGE

There are a wide variety of defenses to a criminal charge. Many of these defenses are specifically mentioned in the Texas Penal Code or the Texas Code of Criminal Procedure (CCrP).[15]

Justifications

A defendant who uses any defense of **justification** admits to committing the crime but also claims that it was necessary to commit the criminal act in order to avoid some greater evil or harm. Justifications that exclude criminal responsibility are discussed in Chapter 9 of the Texas Penal Code. Probably the most well-known justification defense is that of **self-defense**, in which the defendant claims that the use of force against the victim was justifiable because it was the only way the defendant could ensure his or her own safety. Self-defense may involve both deadly and non-deadly force. **Deadly force** is defined as:

> force that is intended or known by the actor to cause, or in the manner of its use or intended use is capable of causing, death or serious bodily injury.[16]

The Penal Law outlines the situations in which the use of force in self-defense is justified, stating that:

> (a) Except as provided in Subsection (b), a person is justified in using force against another when and to the degree he reasonably believes the force is immediately necessary to protect himself against the other's use or attempted use of unlawful force.
> (b) The use of force against another is not justified:
>   (1) in response to verbal provocation alone;
>   (2) to resist an arrest or search that the actor knows is being made by a peace officer, or by a person acting in a peace officer's presence and at his direction, even though the arrest or search is unlawful, unless the resistance is justified under Subsection (c);
>   (3) if the actor consented to the exact force used or attempted by the other;
>   (4) if the actor provoked the other's use or attempted use of unlawful force, unless:
>   (A) the actor abandons the encounter, or clearly communicates to the other his intent to do so reasonably believing he cannot safely abandon the encounter; and
>   (B) the other nevertheless continues or attempts to use unlawful force against the actor; or
>   (5) if the actor sought an explanation from or discussion with the other person concerning the actor's differences with the other person while the actor was:
>   (A) carrying a weapon...; or
>   (B) possessing or transporting a weapon...
> (c) The use of force to resist an arrest or search is justified:
>   (1) if, before the actor offers any resistance, the peace officer (or person acting at his direction) uses or attempts to use greater force than necessary to make the arrest or search; and
>   (2) when and to the degree the actor reasonably believes the force is immediately necessary to protect himself against the peace officer's (or other person's) use or attempted use of greater force than necessary.
> (d) The use of deadly force is not justified under this subchapter except as provided in Sections 9.32, 9.33, and 9.34.[17]

This statute primarily applies to non-deadly force. The last section identifies three specific situations in which deadly force may be used in self-defense. These include:

- in defense of one's self[18]
- in defense of a third person[19]

- in an emergency situation to protect the life of the person against whom force is being used — this section is intended to protect from culpability an individual who provides emergency medical care in an effort to save the life of another person.[20]

The Penal Code also allows for the use of force in the **defense of home and property**. Reasonable force may be used to protect property if the defendant reasonably believes that the force used is necessary at that immediate moment to prevent or stop trespass or illegal interference with property. Force may only be used to recover property if it is used immediately or in fresh pursuit after the property was taken.[21] Deadly force may only be used to protect property under very limited circumstances.[22]

Another justification defense is that of **consent**. This defense claims that the injured person voluntarily consented to the actions that caused the injury. Consent is defined in Pen §1.07(11) as "assent in fact, whether express or apparent." This defense seems to be most commonly used in sex-related offenses, such as sexual assault. For example, the definition of sexual assault specifically states that the actions must be committed without the consent of the other person. The statute makes it clear that coerced consent, obtained through threats of force or violence against the victim or another person, does not constitute a defense of consent.[23]

Excuses

A defendant using an **excuse** defense is claiming that at the time of the criminal act some circumstance or personal condition creates a situation under which s/he should not be held criminally accountable. One defense that falls into this category is that of **duress**. A defendant using this defense claims that s/he was forced by some type of threat to engage in the criminal conduct. The defense is applied differently to felony and misdemeanor offenses. In a felony case, the defendant must show that he or she was compelled to commit the crime by threat of death or serious bodily injury, and also show that the danger was imminent. The burden of proof is on the defendant, who must prove duress by a preponderance of the evidence. In a misdemeanor situation, the defendant only has to show that he or she was compelled to commit the crime by force or threat of force. The requirement of imminency does not apply to a misdemeanor defendant.[24]

The defense of **age** or **infancy** also falls into this category. According to Pen §8.07, individuals may not be prosecuted for, or convicted of, crimes committed when they were under the age of 15, although the statute does list a number of exceptions. The statute also prohibits the imposition of the death penalty on any individual for a crime committed when he or she was under the age of 17. Thus, individuals who are 15 or 16 years of age may be prosecuted for capital murder but may only be sentenced to life imprisonment. There have been some recent unsuccessful legislative attempts in Texas to lower the age limit for the imposition of the death penalty to 16 years of age.

While the old saying that "ignorance of the law is no defense" is true in general, there are some exceptions in Texas, which does allow the defenses of **mistake of law** and **mistake of fact**. Pen §8.02(a) states that,

> It is a defense to prosecution that the actor through mistake formed a reasonable belief about a matter of fact if his mistaken belief negated the kind of culpability required for commission of the offense.

Effectively, criminal intent may be negated if the defendant developed a reasonable but erroneous belief that eliminated the intent. This may not be used as a defense in a case of criminal negligence.

In addition, Pen §8.03 states that,

> (a) It is no defense to prosecution that the actor was ignorant of the provisions of any law after the law has taken effect.
> (b) It is an affirmative defense to prosecution that the actor reasonably believed the conduct charged did not constitute a crime and that he acted in reasonable reliance upon:
> (1) an official statement of the law contained in a written order or grant of permission by an administrative agency charged by law with responsibility for interpreting the law in question; or
> (2) a written interpretation of the law contained in an opinion of a court of record or made by a public official charged by law with responsibility for interpreting the law in question.

Thus, simple ignorance of the law in and of itself is not a defense. However, defendants who mistakenly thought they knew the law, and who based this belief on official statements made by the government or a public official, may be able to use mistake of law as a defense.

Probably the most well-known (and controversial) defense in this category is that of **insanity**. Although the term insanity is no longer used by mental health professionals, it is a legal term referring to a defense that is based on the defendant's claim that he or she was mentally ill or mentally incapacitated at the time of the offense.

Insanity is discussed in Pen §8.01. The statute states that,

> (a) It is an affirmative defense to prosecution that, at the time of the conduct charged, the actor, as a result of severe mental disease or defect, did not know that his conduct was wrong.

It is clear from this section of the statute that Texas uses the **M'Naghten Rule** as a test for insanity.

The procedures involved in the use of the insanity defense are discussed in Article 46.03 of the Texas Code of Criminal Procedure. For the defense of insanity to be used, the defense must give notice of intent to present evidence of insanity at least ten days prior to the date the case is set to come to trial. The burden of proof is on the defendant to prove that he or she did not know that his or her conduct was wrong, because of a severe mental disease or defect. A defendant acquitted of criminal charges using the insanity defense will be found **not guilty by reason of insanity**. However, even though the defendant has been acquitted of the charges, he or she may not be set free, but may be committed for as long as he or she remains mentally ill.

Procedural Defenses

A **procedural defense** claims that some form of official procedure was not followed or that procedural law was not properly followed during the investigation or the prosecution of the crime. One such defense is **entrapment**. Pen §8.06(a) discusses the issue of entrapment, stating that,

> It is a defense to prosecution that the actor engaged in the conduct charged because he was induced to do so by a law enforcement agent using persuasion or other means likely to cause persons to commit the offense. Conduct merely affording a person an opportunity to commit an offense does not constitute entrapment.

The entrapment defense is extremely difficult for the defense to prove. It is most commonly used when the defendant was caught during an undercover police action and seems to be frequently used for crimes involving the sale of illegal drugs. In general, the defendant will claim that s/he does not regularly sell drugs but made the sale as a favor to the undercover officer. One of the most common ways for the police to prevent the use of this defense is to make two or more purchases from the same suspect. After the suspect has made multiple sales, the jury is more likely to believe that the undercover officer simply provided the defendant with an opportunity to commit the crime, rather than that the officer induced or encouraged the defendant to engage in a behavior in which he or she would not normally become involved.

Another procedural defense is the **denial of a speedy trial**. In Texas, the right to a speedy trial is guaranteed in Article I, Section 10, of the Texas Constitution as well as in CCrP Article 1.05. The time limit for a trial to be "speedy" is, in most cases, 60 to 180 days, depending on the seriousness of the offense.[25] This time limit may be extended under certain circumstances. Obviously, if the defendant has requested an extension, s/he may not later claim that his or her right to a speedy trial was denied. However, if the time limit has not been extended by request and if there are no exceptional circumstances which caused a delay, the court must discharge the defendant from custody.

Double jeopardy is another procedural defense. Article I, Section 14, of the Texas Constitution states that,

> No person, for the same offense, shall be twice put in jeopardy of life or liberty, nor shall a person be again put upon trial for the same offense, after a verdict of not guilty in a court of competent jurisdiction.

This statement is repeated in CCrP 1.10. In addition, CCrP 1.11 states that,

> An acquittal of the defendant exempts him from a second trial or a second prosecution for the same offense, however irregular the proceedings may have been; but if the defendant shall have been acquitted upon trial in a court having no jurisdiction of the offense, he may be prosecuted again in a court having jurisdiction.

NOTES

1. The Texas Constitution may be viewed online at http://www.capitol.state.tx.us/txconst/toc.html
2. The home page of the Office of the Governor (http://www.governor.state.tx.us/)
3. Texas Constitution, Article 5, Section 1
4. Texas Constitution, Article 5, Section 2
5. Texas Constitution, Article 5, Section 4
6. Texas Constitution, Article 5, Section 5
7. Texas Constitution, Article 5, Section 6
8. Texas Constitution, Article 5, Section 7
9. Texas Constitution, Article 5, Section 15
10. The Texas Statutes may be viewed online at http://www.capitol.state.tx.us/statutes/statutes.html
11. Pen §12.03(a)
12. Pen §15.01
13. Pen §15.02
14. Pen §15.03 and Pen §15.031
15. The Texas Code of Criminal Procedure may be viewed online at http://www.capitol.state.tx.us/statutes/statutes.html
16. Pen §9.01(3)
17. Pen §9.31
18. Pen §9.32
19. Pen §9.33
20. Pen §9.34
21. Pen §9.41
22. Pen §9.42
23. Pen §22.011
24. Pen §8.05
25. CCrP Art. 32A.02 Sec.1

CHAPTER 3

INDEX CRIMES

INTRODUCTION

The Federal Bureau of Investigation annually publishes the ***Uniform Crime Reports***[1] (UCR), the most widely used source of official data on crime and criminals in the United States. Much of the UCR deals with **index crimes**, a set of eight serious offenses that the FBI uses as a measure of crime in the United States. They are also known as **Part I Offenses**, and include four violent crimes and four property crimes. The eight index crimes measured by the FBI are:

- homicide
- forcible rape
- robbery
- aggravated assault
- burglary
- larceny-theft
- motor vehicle theft
- arson

However, the definitions used by the FBI in compiling the UCR are not always the same as those found in the Texas Penal Code. This chapter will discuss the definitions of these eight serious crimes as provided by the Texas state statutes. As discussed in Chapter 2, all crimes defined in the Texas Penal Code are classified by the seriousness of the crime (for example, manslaughter is a second degree felony). Chapter 12 of the Texas Penal Code discusses ordinary and exceptional punishments for each class of offense. These will be discussed in detail in Chapter 6.

CRIMINAL HOMICIDE

Homicide is the killing of one human being by another. If that killing is illegal, then it is a form of **criminal homicide**. Texas' criminal homicide statute is found in Chapter 19 of the Penal Code. According to Pen §19.01,

> (a) A person commits criminal homicide if he intentionally, knowingly, recklessly, or with criminal negligence causes the death of an individual.
> (b) Criminal homicide is murder, capital murder, manslaughter, or criminally negligent homicide.

Any other type of death is not considered to be a homicide under the Texas statutes.

All the homicide offenses discussed in the Texas Penal Code contain two key elements:

1. conduct that causes the death of an individual

2. the mental culpability of the defendant.

Effectively, these elements are the guilty act (*actus reus*) and the guilty mind (*mens rea*).

The specific homicide offense of which a defendant may be convicted depends on his or her level of mental culpability and on the nature of the circumstances surrounding the death (essentially, the presence or absence of aggravating factors).

The four specific types of criminal homicide are listed in Pen §19.01(b). In addition, Texas also recognizes the crime of felony murder. This is the only type of murder which does not require a direct relationship between the defendant's murderous conduct and his or her the mental state. No intent to commit murder is required for a conviction of felony murder.

Murder

Pen §19.02 discusses the crime of **murder**, stating that:

> (b) A person commits an offense if he:
> (1) intentionally or knowingly causes the death of an individual;
> (2) intends to cause serious bodily injury and commits an act clearly dangerous to human life that causes the death of an individual; or
> (3) commits or attempts to commit a felony, other than manslaughter, and in the course of and in furtherance of the commission or attempt, or in immediate flight from the commission or attempt, he commits or attempts to commit an act clearly dangerous to human life that causes the death of an individual.

Essentially, this statute defines three different types of first degree murder:

1. **Intentional or knowing murder** is the simplest type. The offender who caused the death of another person had the specific and deliberate intent to do so.

2. **Intentional risk of death murder** requires the state to show that the offender intended to cause serious bodily injury to another person and, while voluntarily committing a dangerous act, actually caused the death of the other person. Because the offender does not have to have the

intent to kill, only to cause serious bodily harm, this is a form of transferred intent.

3. **Felony murder** involves an offender who consciously intended to commit a felony (other than manslaughter) and who, during the commission of the felony, caused the death of another person. The intent to commit the *murder is taken from the intent to commit the felony.*

The same statute also defines one type of second degree murder, a **crime of passion**. The statute states that:

> At the punishment stage of a trial, the defendant may raise the issue as to whether he caused the death under the immediate influence of sudden passion arising from an adequate cause. If the defendant proves the issue in the affirmative by a preponderance of the evidence, the offense is a felony of the second degree.[2]

Essentially, if the offender is found guilty of first degree murder and can then show, at the punishment stage of the trial, that the crime was committed in the heat of passion, the crime is reduced to voluntary manslaughter and punished as a second degree felony.

First degree murder is punishable by imprisonment in a state prison for life or for a term of not less than five years nor more than 99 years.

Capital Murder

The general murder statute defines murder as a first degree felony. First degree felonies are not punishable by death. However, under some circumstances, criminal homicide becomes a capital felony, which is punishable either by life imprisonment or by a sentence of death. **Capital murder** includes two key elements:

1. the *offender intentionally or knowingly* causes the death of another person (intentional or knowing murder), and

2. at least one aggravating factor is present.

There are eight aggravating factors listed in the statutes that elevate first degree murder to capital murder. They are listed in Pen §19.03(a):

> (1) the person murders a peace officer or fireman who is acting in the lawful discharge of an official duty and who the person knows is a peace officer or fireman;
> (2) the person intentionally commits the murder in the course of committing or attempting to commit kidnapping, burglary, robbery, aggravated sexual assault, arson, obstruction or retaliation, or terroristic threat...;

(3) the person commits the murder for remuneration or the promise of remuneration or employs another to commit the murder for remuneration or the promise of remuneration;
(4) the person commits the murder while escaping or attempting to escape from a penal institution;
(5) the person, while incarcerated in a penal institution, murders another:
    (A) who is employed in the operation of the penal institution; or
    (B) with the intent to establish, maintain, or participate in a combination or in the profits of a combination;
(6) the person:
    (A) while incarcerated for an offense under this section or Section 19.02, murders another; or
    (B) while serving a sentence of life imprisonment or a term of 99 years for an offense under Section 20.04, 22.021, or 29.03, murders another;
(7) the person murders more than one person:
    (A) during the same criminal transaction; or
    (B) during different criminal transactions but the murders are committed pursuant to the same scheme or course of conduct; or
(8) the person murders an individual under six years of age.

If none of these aggravating factors are present, the offender may still be convicted of murder or some other lesser offense. However, the offender may not be sentenced to the death penalty. Capital murder is the only death penalty offense in Texas. The topic of capital punishment is discussed in more detail in Chapter 7.

Manslaughter

Manslaughter occurs when the offender "recklessly causes the death of an individual."[3] Essentially, the offender is involved in some action, knows that there is a clear risk of death to another person as a result of this action, and deliberately disregards that risk in a situation when a reasonable person would not disregard it. Actual intent to kill is not a required element of this crime. In fact, there is no crime of attempted manslaughter in Texas because by definition an attempt requires the presence of intent.

Manslaughter is a second degree felony in Texas, calling for a term of incarceration in a state prison for a term of not less than two nor more than twenty years.

Criminally Negligent Homicide

Criminally negligent homicide is the lowest category of homicide in Texas. An offender commits the crime of criminally negligent homicide "if he causes the death of an individual by criminal negligence."[4] The key difference between criminally negligent homicide and manslaughter is the culpable mental state that is required as an element of the crime. While neither offense requires a deliberate intent to kill, manslaughter involves behavior that is committed recklessly and criminally negligent homicide only involves criminal negligence. Criminal negligence is defined as:

> A person acts with criminal negligence, or is criminally negligent, with respect to circumstances surrounding his conduct or the result of his conduct when he ought to be aware of a substantial and unjustifiable risk that the circumstances exist or the result will occur. The risk must be of such a nature and degree that the failure to perceive it constitutes a gross deviation from the standard of care that an ordinary person would exercise under all the circumstances as viewed from the actor's standpoint.[5]

In criminally negligent homicide, the offender does not perceive a risk that any reasonable person would perceive. There is no crime of attempted negligent homicide as the crime by definition does not involve any intent to kill.

In Texas, criminally negligent homicide is frequently the charge used in cases of fatal motor vehicle accidents that do not involve drugs or alcohol but that do involve one or more aggravating negligent factors, such as speeding or tailgating during rush hour. The crime is a state jail felony, punishable by incarceration in a state jail facility for a term of not less than 180 days or more than two years.

FORCIBLE RAPE

In the Uniform Crime Reporting Program, forcible rape is defined as "the carnal knowledge of a female forcibly and against her will."[6] This originally reflected the prevailing definitions used in many states in the United States. However, during the 1980s and 1990s, the Texas Penal Code relating to sexual offenses was significantly revised. The crimes of "rape," "sexual abuse," "rape of a child", and "statutory rape" were reclassified from sexual offenses to assaultive offenses. In addition, the marital exemption clause, which excluded spouses as victims of sexual assaults, was eliminated. Therefore, offenders who rape or sexually abuse their spouses may no longer use their marital state as a defense.

Chapter 21 of the Texas Penal Law is entitled "Sexual Offenses," but it includes crimes such as public lewdness, indecent exposure, indecency with a child, and homosexual conduct. Assaultive crimes, including crimes of sexual assault, are discussed in Chapter 22 of the Texas Penal Law, which currently includes two main types of "rape":

- sexual assault
- aggravated sexual assault

Sexual assault is defined in Pen §22.011(a). The statute states that:

> A person commits an offense if the person:
> (1) intentionally or knowingly:

(A) causes the penetration of the anus or female sexual organ of another person by any means, without that person's consent;
(B) causes the penetration of the mouth of another person by the sexual organ of the actor, without that person's consent; or
(C) causes the sexual organ of another person, without that person's consent, to contact or penetrate the mouth, anus, or sexual organ of another person, including the actor; or

(2) intentionally or knowingly:
(A) causes the penetration of the anus or female sexual organ of a child by any means;
(B) causes the penetration of the mouth of a child by the sexual organ of the actor;
(C) causes the sexual organ of a child to contact or penetrate the mouth, anus, or sexual organ of another person, including the actor;
(D) causes the anus of a child to contact the mouth, anus, or sexual organ of another person, including the actor; or
(E) causes the mouth of a child to contact the anus or sexual organ of another person, including the actor.

This statute includes two specific types of behavior. The first involves non-consensual intercourse of various types between adults, regardless of their marital status.[7] The second involves any intercourse, regardless of whether or not consent was given, between an adult and a child. A child is defined by Pen §22.011(c)(1) as an individual who is less than 17 years of age and who is not the spouse of the person committing the offense. This creates an exception to the crime: sexual relations that involves spouses, when one or both are below the age of 17, do not fall under this statute.

The most commonly used defenses to sexual assault of an adult victim are consent and lack of penetration. By definition, consent is not a defense against intercourse with a child. However, Pen §22.011(e) states that if the offender is no more than three years older than the victim and the victim is at least 14 years of age, the defendant has an affirmative defense against the crime.

Sexual assault is a second degree felony.

Aggravated sexual assault is defined in Pen §22.021(a). The statute states that:

A person commits an offense:
(1) if the person:
(A) intentionally or knowingly:
(i) causes the penetration of the anus or female sexual organ of another person by any means, without that person's consent;
(ii) causes the penetration of the mouth of another person by the sexual organ of the actor, without that person's consent; or

(iii) causes the sexual organ of another person, without that person's consent, to contact or penetrate the mouth, anus, or sexual organ of another person, including the actor; or

(B) intentionally or knowingly:

(i) causes the penetration of the anus or female sexual organ of a child by any means;

(ii) causes the penetration of the mouth of a child by the sexual organ of the actor;

(iii) causes the sexual organ of a child to contact or penetrate the mouth, anus, or sexual organ of another person, including the actor;

(iv) causes the anus of a child to contact the mouth, anus, or sexual organ of another person, including the actor; or

(v) causes the mouth of a child to contact the anus or sexual organ of another person, including the actor; and

(2) if:

(A) the person:

(I) causes serious bodily injury or attempts to cause the death of the victim or another person in the course of the same criminal episode;

(ii) by acts or words places the victim in fear that death, serious bodily injury, or kidnapping will be imminently inflicted on any person;

(iii) by acts or words occurring in the presence of the victim threatens to cause the death, serious bodily injury, or kidnapping of any person;

(iv) uses or exhibits a deadly weapon in the course of the same criminal episode;

(v) acts in concert with another who engages in conduct described by Subdivision (1) directed toward the same victim and occurring during the course of the same criminal episode; or

(vi) administers or provides flunitrazepam, otherwise known as rohypnol, or gamma hydroxbutyrate to the victim of the offense with the intent of facilitating the commission of the offense;

(B) the victim is younger than 14 years of age; or

(C) the victim is an elderly individual or a disabled individual.

The first part of this statute is virtually identical to the sexual assault statute outlined above. The second part lists a number of aggravating factors that make the crime more serious than sexual assault. The first group of aggravating factors all involve the behavior of the offender. These include causing serious bodily injury to the victim, placing the victim in fear of death or serious bodily injury, placing the victim in fear of death or serious bodily injury to a third person, using or showing a deadly weapon, gang rape, and the use of "date rape" drugs such as rohypnol or GHB. The remaining factors focus on the status of the victim, specifically the victim's age. The crime is elevated from sexual assault to aggravated sexual assault if the victim is less than 14 years old, is at least 65 years of age (the definition of "elderly"), or is disabled.

Aggravated sexual assault is a first degree felony.

ROBBERY

The Uniform Crime Reporting Program defines **robbery** as "the taking or attempting to take anything of value from the care, custody, or control of a person or persons by force or threat of force or violence and/or by putting the victim in fear."[8] Texas recognizes two categories of this crime: robbery and aggravated robbery. Pen §29.02(a) defines **robbery** as:

> A person commits an offense if, in the course of committing theft ... and with intent to obtain or maintain control of the property, he:
> (1) intentionally, knowingly, or recklessly causes bodily injury to another; or
> (2) intentionally or knowingly threatens or places another in fear of imminent bodily injury or death.

The phrase, "in the course of committing theft", includes any behavior that occurs during an attempt to commit a theft, during the actual commission of a theft, or during the immediate flight from the theft or attempted theft. Property includes,

> (A) tangible or intangible personal property including anything severed from land; or
> (B) a document, including money, that represents or embodies anything of value.[9]

Thus, in Texas, robbery basically involves some type of assaultive behavior that occurs during one of three situations:

1. during the commission of a theft
2. during an attempted theft
3. during the offender's immediate flight after committing or attempting to commit a theft

Robbery essentially is a combination of assault and theft. It is a crime that involves the use of force or fear to illegally obtain the personal property of another person. The key difference between robbery and theft is the presence of the assaultive conduct, while the key difference between robbery and assault is the attempt to acquire the property of another. For the crime of robbery to be proved, some connection must be shown between the assaultive behavior and the theft, so that the assault was committed specifically for the purpose of committing the theft or escaping after the theft.

Some states, such as New York, require an actual theft or larceny as an element of the crime of robbery. However, in Texas, this is not the case. Even if no property is actually taken, the defendant may be found guilty of robbery if it can be shown that s/he attempted to take the property of another. Specific intent to obtain the property of another, even if the property was not actually obtained, is sufficient.

The use of force or the threat of force is also a required element of robbery. In addition, the offender must have intended the assaultive conduct. In the case of actual bodily harm, the level of intent may be intentional, knowingly, or recklessly. In the case of threat or fear, the level of intent may be intentionally or knowingly (but not recklessly). The threat does not need to be verbal; threats implied by the offender's conduct are sufficient to meet the statutory requirement.

According to the case of *Yarbrough v. State*,[10] the victim who is assaulted or threatened with force does not have to be the same person as the intended victim of the theft. If the offender commits or attempts to commit a theft and then, while escaping from the scene, injures a bystander, the offender may still be guilty of the crime of robbery. However, in *Thompson v. State*,[11] the court stated that it is necessary for the state to show that there is some relationship or connection between the theft and the violent behavior. Thus, an individual who discovers an assault victim and steals the victim's property is not guilty of the crime of robbery (although s/he may be guilty of theft).

Aggravated robbery is essentially a robbery that includes one or more statutorily identified aggravating factors. The crime is defined in Pen §29.03(a), which states that:

> A person commits an offense if he commits robbery as defined in Section 29.02, and he:
> (1) causes serious bodily injury to another;
> (2) uses or exhibits a deadly weapon; or
> (3) causes bodily injury to another person or threatens or places another person in fear of imminent bodily injury or death, if the other person is:
> (A) 65 years of age or older; or
> (B) a disabled person.

The first two aggravating factors involve behaviors of the offender: causing serious bodily injury to the victim while committing the robbery, or using or displaying a deadly weapon in the course of the robbery. The third factor focuses on the status of the victim: the crime is considered more serious if the victim is disabled or elderly. However, this factor only applies to the victim of the assaultive behavior. If the elderly or disabled individual is the victim of the underlying theft, but not the violence, the offender is not guilty of aggravated robbery.

Bodily injury is defined as "physical pain, illness, or any impairment of physical condition."[12] Serious bodily injury is defined as

> bodily injury that creates a substantial risk of death or that causes death, serious permanent disfigurement, or protracted loss or impairment of the function of any bodily member or organ.[13]

The difference between bodily injury and serious bodily injury is often difficult to distinguish and frequently requires the use of expert testimony.

Aggravated robbery is a first degree felony.

AGGRAVATED ASSAULT

There is often some confusion about the actual meaning of **assault**. In many states, assault does not involve the infliction of any injury upon another person, it is merely the intentional attempt or threat to cause injury. In these states, when an injury is actually inflicted, a **battery** has occurred. The Uniform Crime Reporting Program defines aggravated assault as:

> an unlawful attack by one person upon another for the purpose of inflicting severe or aggravated bodily injury. This type of assault is usually accompanied by the use of a weapon or by means likely to produce death or great bodily harm.[14]

In Texas, however, one of the possible elements of assault is the infliction of some type of bodily injury to another person. Thus, there is no crime of battery in Texas.

The crime of assault is discussed in Chapter 22 of the Texas Penal Code, which includes both assault and aggravated assault. As with many other crimes defined in the Penal Code, the more serious offense includes all the elements of the lesser offense with the addition of one or more aggravating factors.

Pen §22.0(a) defines the crime of **assault**, stating that:

> A person commits an offense if the person:
> (1) intentionally, knowingly, or recklessly causes bodily injury to another, including the person's spouse;
> (2) intentionally or knowingly threatens another with imminent bodily injury, including the person's spouse; or
> (3) intentionally or knowingly causes physical contact with another when the person knows or should reasonably believe that the other will regard the contact as offensive or provocative.

Thus, this statute essentially includes three specific types of behavior, all of which are considered to be assault:

1. actually causing bodily injury to a victim

2. threatening the victim with bodily injury, but not actually inflicting any injury

3. physically contacting the victim in a way that the offender knows will be considered offensive or provocative

One of the key elements of assault is the culpable mental state of the offender. The law considers assault to have occurred when an injury was committed intentionally, knowingly, or recklessly. If the assault consisted of a threat of injury or of offensive or provocative physical contact, the offender's *mental state must* be at the level of intentional or knowing.

In most cases, assault that involves actual physical harm to the victim is a Class A misdemeanor. However, according to Pen §22.01(b), the crime becomes a third degree felony if the victim falls into one of the following categories:

1. The victim is a public servant and the assault was committed either while the victim was involved in lawful official duties or in retaliation for the performance of such duties.

2. The victim is a member of the offender's family or household and the offender has a prior conviction for assault against a member of his or her family or household.

3. The victim is an individual who contracts with the government to perform a service in a correctional facility.

The second condition is a relatively new change in the Penal Code. Prior to September 1, 1999, repeat family violence of this type was raised to the level of a state jail felony, not a third degree felony. In addition, the elevation of punishment used to require at least two prior convictions; currently one prior conviction or a deferred adjudication will lead to the enhanced punishment. The third condition was added in 2003 because of the increasing privatization of some aspects of corrections in Texas.

Assault that involves offensive touching or the threat of bodily harm is generally a Class C misdemeanor. However, the crime becomes a Class A misdemeanor if the victim is disabled or at least 65 years of age.[15]

Aggravated assault is defined in Pen §22.02(a), which states that

> A person commits an offense if the person commits assault ... and the person:
> (1) causes serious bodily injury to another, including the person's spouse; or
> (2) uses or exhibits a deadly weapon during the commission of the assault.

Essentially, this is simple assault with the presence of at least one of two additional aggravating elements, the infliction of serious bodily harm and/or the use or exhibition of a deadly weapon while committing the assault. The statute was revised in 1994 to include the element of exhibiting a deadly weapon. Prior to that time, only the actual use of a deadly weapon was sufficient to elevate the crime from simple to aggravated assault.

Because of the first condition (serious bodily injury), there is often a very fine line between simple and aggravated assault, depending on the exact nature of the injury sustained by the victim. There is a considerable amount of case law in Texas discussing the definition of serious bodily injury.

In most cases, aggravated assault is a second degree felony. However, as with simple assault, penalty enhancements are provided for in certain situations. According to Pen §22.02(b), the crime becomes a first degree felony if one of the following conditions applies:

1. The offender is a public servant who is acting under color of his or her office.

2. The victim is a public servant and the assault was committed either while the victim was involved in lawful official duties or in retaliation for the performance of such duties.

3. The victim was assaulted because s/he served as a witness, prospective witness, or informant, or because s/he reported a crime.

4. The victim is a security officer performing work-related duties.

For those conditions that involve a victim who is employed in a specific capacity, the offender must know the status of the victim. In other words, if the victim is a security officer engaged in performing his or her duties at the time of the assault, but the offender is unaware of this fact, then the crime is not elevated to a first degree felony. If the victim is wearing a uniform or badge indicating employment as a public servant or security officer, the offender is presumed to be aware of the victim's status.[16]

BURGLARY

In common law, the crime of **burglary** was defined as the breaking and entering of a dwelling at night with intent to commit a felony. Today, the definition of burglary includes structures other than a dwelling place, can occur during the daytime as well as at night, and can involve either an intended felony or misdemeanor. The Uniform Crime Reporting Program defines burglary as the "unlawful entry of a structure to commit a felony or theft."[17]

In Texas, burglary statutes are found in Chapter 30 of the Penal Code. According to Pen §30.02(a):

> A person commits an offense if, without the effective consent of the owner, he:
> (1) enters a habitation, or a building (or any portion of a building) not then open to the public, with intent to commit a felony, theft, or an assault; or
> (2) remains concealed, with intent to commit a felony, theft, or an assault, in a building or habitation; or
> (3) enters a building or habitation and commits or attempts to commit a felony, theft, or an assault.

The actual conduct that the offender is required to commit varies with the sections of the statute. For the first two types of burglary, the actual felony, theft, or assault does not have to actually take place and the state is not required to prove the elements of the underlying crime. Only the intent to commit the crime is required. Basically, once the offender enters the building or habitation with intent, the crime of burglary is completed, even if the underlying felony, theft, or assault is never committed or attempted.[18] However, for the third type of burglary the state must prove that the underlying crime was actually committed or attempted.

The level of intent required also varies with the sections of the statute. For the first type of burglary, the state must prove entry with specific intent to commit a felony, theft, or assault. For the other two types of burglary, the state is not required to prove that the offender, at the time s/he entered the building or habitation, had specific intent to commit the underlying crime. However, for the second type of burglary listed above, the state must show that the offender remained hidden in the location with intent to commit the felony, theft, or assault.

Several types of burglary include the element of entry. Entry occurs when any part of the offender's body or any physical object that is connected with the offender's body crosses or intrudes into the plane of the structure.[19] Presence just outside a door does not constitute entry. However, reaching an arm or something held in the hand through a window is sufficient to establish entry. Unlawful entry occurs when the defendant is not licensed or privileged to enter. In some situations, a burglary may even occur if the owner of the building invited the offender into the building or in some other way gave the offender permission to enter. The permission to enter is canceled or nullified by the criminal intent of the burglar. Therefore, an individual who enters the location at a time when it was open to the public but remains within after the termination of this legal right may be guilty of burglary. For example, an offender who enters a store while it is open to the public, and remains concealed in the store after it has closed, meets the criteria for unlawful entry.

For the crime to be considered a burglary under Texas laws, the location must be a building or a habitation. Pen §30.01 defines these terms:

> (1) "Habitation" means a structure or vehicle that is adapted for the overnight accommodation of persons, and includes:
> (A) each separately secured or occupied portion of the structure or vehicle; and
> (B) each structure appurtenant to or connected with the structure or vehicle.
>
> (2) "Building" means any enclosed structure intended for use or occupation as a habitation or for some purpose of trade, manufacture, ornament, or use.

Basically, a habitation includes homes, apartments, and motor homes, as well as any attached buildings and garages. A building is a more general term. The statute includes the term "enclosed," which allows the courts to consider structures such as sheds and barns on a case-by-case basis.

The penalty for burglary depends on the characteristics of the crime and of the structure that was targeted. The burglary of any building that is not a habitation (for example, a business of some type) is a state jail felony. The burglary of a habitation with intent to steal is a second degree felony. The burglary of a habitation with intent to commit (or the attempt or actual commission of) any crime other than felony theft (for example, assault) is a first degree felony.[20]

The Texas Penal Code also recognizes two other specific types of burglary, which do not involve buildings or habitations. Pen §30.03(a) discusses the **burglary of coin-operated or coin collection machines**. This crime, which is a Class A misdemeanor, is defined as:

> A person commits an offense if, without the effective consent of the owner, he breaks or enters into any coin-operated machine, coin collection machine, or other coin-operated or coin collection receptacle, contrivance, apparatus, or equipment used for the purpose of providing lawful amusement, sales of goods, services, or other valuable things, or telecommunications with intent to obtain property or services.

In addition, Pen §30.04(a) defines the **burglary of a vehicle**, stating that:

> A person commits an offense if, without the effective consent of the owner, he breaks into or enters a vehicle or any part of a vehicle with intent to commit any felony or theft.

In most cases, this crime is a Class A misdemeanor. However, if the vehicle or part of vehicle that was broken into was a rail car, or a container or trailer carried on a rail car, the crime is a state jail felony. A "vehicle is defined as:

> any device in, on, or by which any person or property is or may be propelled, moved, or drawn in the normal course of commerce or transportation, except such devices as are classified as "habitation."[21]

It includes not only automobiles but also items such as trucks, buses, railway cars, golf carts, tractors, boats, jet skis, bicycles, and mobile homes that have not been secured for use as habitation.

LARCENY-THEFT

The Uniform Crime Reporting Program defines **larceny-theft** as:

> the unlawful taking, carrying, leading, or riding away of property from the possession or constructive possession of another. It includes crimes such as shoplifting, pocket-picking, purse-snatching, thefts from motor vehicles, thefts of motor vehicle parts and accessories, bicycle thefts, etc., in which no use of force, violence, or fraud occurs.[22]

Prior to 1974, Texas had a large number of crimes that were theft-related. However, in 1974, Pen §31.02 consolidated most of these into the single crime of theft. These crimes, which were separate offenses prior to the passage of this statute, include theft, theft by false pretext, conversion by a bailee, theft from the person, shoplifting acquisition of property by threat, swindling, swindling by worthless check, embezzlement, extortion, receiving or concealing embezzled property, and receiving or concealing stolen property.

Pen §31.03, which discusses the crime of theft, is extremely long and detailed. The basic offense itself is defined in section (a) of the statute, which states that a theft occurs when a person "unlawfully appropriates property with intent to deprive the owner of property." Essentially, the crime has two elements:

1. The offender must appropriate the property unlawfully.
2. The offender must have intent to deprive the owner of the property.

Section (b) of the statute outlines when appropriation of property is unlawful. This occurs when any one of the following conditions is met:

1. The property is taken without the owner's effective consent.
2. The offender knowingly appropriates property that was stolen by another person.
3. The property is in the custody of a law enforcement agency, the offender was specifically told that the property was stolen, and the offender appropriates the property while believing it was stolen by another person.

The second condition is essentially the former "receiving stolen property" statute and allows the state to more easily prosecute offenders for the offense of fencing. In fact, a considerable portion of section (c) of the statute focuses on various types of evidence aimed at the prosecution of fencing cases.

According to Pen §31.01(5), property can include any of the following:

(A) real property;
(B) tangible or intangible personal property including anything severed from land; or
(C) a document, including money, that represents or embodies anything of value.

The penalty for the crime of theft depends primarily on the value of the property that was stolen. Section (e) of the statute goes into detail about the different classifications of the crime. Essentially, the crime of theft is classified as:

1. A Class C misdemeanor if the value of the property stolen is less than $50

2. A Class B misdemeanor if the value of the property stolen is at least $50 but less than $500 or the value is less than $50 and the defendant has a prior conviction for theft

3. A Class A misdemeanor if the value of the property stolen is at least $500 but less than $1,500

4. A state jail felony if the value of the property stolen is at least $1,500 but less than $20,000, or the value is less than $1,500 and the defendant has two or more prior theft convictions. In addition, the theft is considered a state jail felony if the property was stolen from the person of another, or from a human corpse or grave, or if the property was a firearm, an official election ballot or carrier envelope, or if the property stolen included certain specified livestock or exotic fowl

5. A felony of the third degree if the value of the property stolen is at least $20,000 but less than $100,000 or if the property includes certain specified livestock or exotic fowl

6. A felony of the second degree if the value of the property stolen is at least $100,000 but less than $200,000
7. A felony of the first degree if the value of the property stolen is at least $200,000

In addition, Pen §31.03(f) states that any theft (except a theft which is classified as a first degree felony) will be increased by one level if it can be shown that the offender was a public servant or government contractor and that the offender obtained the property because of this status, or if the owner of the property was elderly.

In a separate statute, Texas also recognized the crime of theft of service. Pen §31.04(a) states that:

> A person commits theft of service if, with intent to avoid payment for service that he knows is provided only for compensation:
> (1) he intentionally or knowingly secures performance of the service by deception, threat, or false token;
> (2) having control over the disposition of services of another to which he is not entitled, he intentionally or knowingly diverts the other's services to his own benefit or to the benefit of another not entitled to them; or
> (3) having control of personal property under a written rental agreement, he holds the property beyond the expiration of the rental period without the effective consent of the owner of the property, thereby depriving the owner of the property of its use in further rentals; or
> (4) he intentionally or knowingly secures the performance of the service by agreeing to provide compensation and, after the service is rendered, fails to make payment after receiving notice demanding payment.

The main purpose of this statute is to outlaw the unlawful taking of something that does not fall under the basic definition of property. Service is defined in Pen §31.01(6) and includes labor and professional services, various public utility, transportation, and telecommunication services, lodging, restaurant service, entertainment, and property and motor vehicle rental. As with theft of property, the seriousness of this crime is determined by the value of the service stolen:

1. The crime is a Class C misdemeanor if the value of the service stolen is less than $20

2. The crime is a Class B misdemeanor if the value of the service stolen is at least $20 but less than $500.

3. The crime is a Class A misdemeanor if the value of the service stolen is at least $500 but less than $1,500.

4. The crime is a state jail felony if the value of the service stolen is at least $1,500 but less than $20,000.

5. The crime is a third degree felony if the value of the service stolen is at least $20,00 but less than $100,000.

6. The crime is a second degree felony if the value of the service stolen is at least $100,000 but less than $200,000.

7. The crime is a first degree felony if the value of the service stolen is at least $200,000.[23]

MOTOR VEHICLE THEFT

The Uniform Crime Reporting Program considers **motor vehicle theft** to be a separate index crime from larceny-theft. It is defined by the FBI as:

> the theft or attempted theft of a motor vehicle, this offense category includes the stealing of automobiles, trucks, buses, motorcycles, motorscooters, snowmobiles, etc.[24]

Texas does not consider motor vehicle theft to be a separate crime from theft. The statutory definition of theft includes the theft of any tangible personal property.[25] This includes the theft of a motor vehicle.

Pen §31.07 does discuss the crime of the **unauthorized use of a vehicle**. The statute states that:

> (a) A person commits an offense if he intentionally or knowingly operates another's boat, airplane, or motor-propelled vehicle without the effective consent of the owner.
> (b) An offense under this section is a state jail felony.

This statute effectively outlaws "joyriding." Actual operation of the vehicle is a necessary element of the crime. Merely entering the vehicle without the owner's consent does not meet the statutory definition of the crime. The statute does not require the prosecution to show that the offender intended to deprive the owner of the vehicle.

ARSON

Like burglary, the common-law felony crime of **arson** was a crime against a home or dwelling place. While it could occur at any time of day, nighttime arson was considered to be a more serious crime. The Uniform Crime Reporting Program defines arson as:

> any willful or malicious burning or attempt to burn, with or without intent to defraud, a dwelling house, public building, motor vehicle or aircraft, personal property of another, etc.[26]

In Texas, the burning of other types of property is also recognized as arson. Arson in defined in Pen §28.02, which states that:

> (a) A person commits an offense if the person starts a fire, regardless of whether the fire continues after ignition, or causes an explosion with intent to destroy or damage:
> (1) any vegetation, fence, or structure on open-space land; or
> (2) any building, habitation, or vehicle:
> (A) knowing that it is within the limits of an incorporated city or town;
> (B) knowing that it is insured against damage or destruction;
> (C) knowing that it is subject to a mortgage or other security interest;
> (D) knowing that it is located on property belonging to another;
> (E) knowing that it has located within it property belonging to another; or
> (F) when the person is reckless about whether the burning or explosion will endanger the life of some individual or the safety of the property of another.
> (b) It is an exception to the application of Subsection (a)(1) that the fire or explosion was a part of the controlled burning of open-space land.

The definitions of the terms "building," "habitation," and "vehicle" are identical to the definitions used in the burglary statute.

A key element of the crime of arson is specific intent to destroy or damage some type of property. Therefore, careless behavior that results in a fire (for example, shooting off fireworks during a drought) is not arson under the statute. In addition, obtaining a permit for a fire from the state prior to starting the fire is a defense against prosecution for the crime of arson. However, actual damage or destruction is not required to prove the crime of arson, only that there was intent. According to *Romo v. State*[27], if the offender intended to damage or destroy property, the offense is completed when the fire is set or the explosion occurs, regardless of whether any damage or destruction actually occurs.

In most cases, arson is a second degree felony. However, according to Pen §28.02(d), the crime is elevated to a first degree felony if one of two conditions applies. First, if the offense resulted in bodily injury or death to any person, the crime is considered to be more serious. The definition of bodily injury has been hotly debated in the courts and may even include smoke inhalation. Second, if the offender committed the crime knowing that the property targeted was a habitation or place of assembly or worship, the seriousness of the crime is increased. The section of this statute that deals with the arson of a place of worship was added to the statute in 1997, in response to the burning of a number of churches throughout Texas and other southern states. The section relating to habitations and places of assembly was added in 2001.

HATE CRIMES

Hate or bias crimes are not specifically included among the eight index crimes. However, the FBI began to collect data on this category of crime after President Bush signed the Hate Crimes Statistics Act in 1990. The Uniform Crime Reporting Program defines hate or bias crimes as "those offenses motivated in part or singularly by personal prejudice against others because of a diversity—race, sexual orientation, religion, ethnicity/national origin, or disability.[28]

Section 411.046 of the Government Code, the **Texas Hate Crime Reporting Act**, defines hate crimes as "crimes that are motivated by prejudice, hatred, or advocacy of violence..." The Act requires all law enforcement agencies in Texas to report hate or bias crimes to the Texas Department of Public Safety (DPS). The DPS is required to maintain and disseminate records and statistics on hate crimes in the state.

In 2002, there were a total of 344 hate crime incidents reported in Texas, a decrease of 19.8 percent from the previous year. The 344 reported incidents resulted in a total of 363 offenses that involved 429 victims and 470 offenders. The most common crimes were vandalism (28 percent), simple assault (27 percent), intimidation (19 percent), and aggravated assault (15 percent). There was one murder motivated by bias in 2002.[29]

The most frequent motivation was racial; approximately 53 percent of the reported hate crimes were motivated by the race or color of the victim. Other motivations included the victim's ethnicity or national origin (23 percent), sexual orientation (15 percent), and religion (8 percent). There were a very small number of hate crimes (less than 1 percent) motivated by a physical disability of the victim.[30]

Approximately 48 percent of hate crime offenders were white, 20 percent were black, and 3 percent were of other races. The race of almost 30 percent of hate crime offenders was unknown. Almost all hate crimes committed in 2002 (96 percent) were directed against individual victims. Other targets included businesses, governments, and religious organizations. The most common location for a hate crime in Texas in 2002 was a home or residence, with approximately 38 percent of reported hate crimes occurring at home. Approximately 20 percent of the hate crimes occurred on highways, streets, roads, or alleys, and almost 16 percent occurred in parking lots and garages.[31]

Pen §12.47 mandates sentencing enhancements if a crime was committed because of bias or prejudice. The statute states that:

> (a) If an affirmative finding under Article 42.014, Code of Criminal Procedure, is made in the punishment phase of the trial of an offense other than a first degree felony or a Class A misdemeanor, the punishment for the offense is increased to the punishment prescribed for the next highest category of offense. If the offense is a Class A misdemeanor, the minimum term of confinement for the offense is increased to 180 days. This section does not apply to the trial of a disabled

> individual ... , if the affirmative finding in the case ... shows that the defendant intentionally selected the victim because the victim was disabled.

This statute, as well as CCrP §42.014, were revised by the 2001 Legislature. The former version of Pen §12.47 was originally enacted in 1993 and is still valid for offenses committed prior to September 1, 2001. The current version is narrower and applies only to those crimes specifically mentioned in the new version of CCrP §42.014. These include all crimes found in Title 5 of the Penal Code (Offenses Against the Person)[32] as well as arson, criminal mischief, and graffiti. The former version of CCrP $42.014 applied to all offenses under the Penal Code. The revised version of CCrP §42.014 also moved the issue of motivation by bias or prejudice into the guilt-or-innocence phase of the trial, rather than the punishment phase.

NOTES

1. Recent issues of the *Uniform Crime Reports* may be viewed online on the Federal Bureau of Investigation's website (http://www.fbi.gov/ucr/ucr.htm)
2. Pen §19.02(d)
3. Pen §19.04(a)
4. Pen §19.05(a)
5. Pen §6.03(d)
6. *Uniform Crime Reports, op cit.*
7. The circumstances required for a sexual assault to be non-consensual are listed in Pen §22.011(b)
8. *Uniform Crime Reports, op cit.*
9. Pen §29.01(2)
10. *Yarbrough v. State* 656 S.W.2d 200 (Tex. App. - Austin 1983, no pet.)
11. *Thompson v. State*, 650 S.W.2d (156 (Tex. App - Houston [14th Dist.] 1983, no pet.)
12. Pen §1.07(a)(8)
13. Pen. §1.07(a)(46)
14. *Uniform Crime Reports, op cit.*
15. Pen §22.01(c)
16. Pen §22.02(c)
17. *Uniform Crime Reports, op cit.*
18. See e.g., *Stearn v. State*, 571 S.W.2d 177 (Tex. Crim. App. 1978)
19. Pen §30.02(b)
20. Pen §30.02(c) and Pen §30.02(d)
21. Pen §30.01(3)
22. *Uniform Crime Reports, op cit.*
23. Pen §31.04(e)
24. *Uniform Crime Reports, op cit.*
25. Pen §31.03
26. *Uniform Crime Reports, op cit.*
27. *Romo v. State*, 593 S.W.2d 690 (Tex. Crim. App. 1980)

28. *Uniform Crime Reports, op cit.*
29. Texas Department of Public Safety (2001). *The Texas Crime Report for 2002*. Available online at: http://www.txdps.state.tx.us/crimereports/citindex.htm
30. *Ibid*
31. *Ibid*
32. Title 5 includes Chapter 19 (Criminal Homicide), Chapter 20 (Kidnapping and Unlawful Restraint), Chapter 21 (Sexual Offenses), and Chapter 22 (Assaultive Offenses)

CHAPTER 4

THE POLICE IN TEXAS

INTRODUCTION

There are many levels of police agencies in America, including federal law enforcement, state police, county sheriffs' agencies, and city police. Texas' location, particularly its proximity to Mexico, creates a number of special law enforcement problems, particularly revolving around issues such as drugs, immigration, and tourism. Because of this, a large number of federal law enforcement agencies have offices in Texas and/or are involved in law enforcement activities within the state. These include the Federal Bureau of Investigation; the Drug Enforcement Agency; the Immigration and Naturalization Service; U.S. Customs; the Bureau of Alcohol, Tobacco, and Firearms; the U.S. Coast Guard; and the U.S. Border Patrol. This results in a considerable amount of overlap among the various levels of law enforcement in the state.

LOCAL POLICING

The majority of police departments in Texas are **local or city departments**. Currently, most local cities, towns, and villages in Texas maintain police departments. Every local department is independent of every other department. The goals, purposes, and priorities vary greatly among departments, with each local agency responding to the needs and desires of the population it serves. Sizes range from small departments with less than five full-time officers to large urban agencies with thousands of sworn officers.

Municipal police departments in Texas are full-service police agencies which provide a wide range of police services, including law enforcement, order maintenance, and service. The chief or director of each department generally is appointed by the head of the city's political system.

The Houston Police Department

Houston is the largest city in Texas and the fourth largest city in the United States.[1] The **Houston Police Department** (HPD) is currently the largest local police department in the state. In 2002, the department employed 5,360 sworn officers and 1,724 civilians.[2]

The HPD is divided into a number of **Commands**, each of which has a specific area of responsibility. Each is headed by an Assistant Chief or Civilian Director, depending on the functions and duties of the Command. Patrol responsibilities are divided among the **North Patrol Command** and the **South Patrol Command**. Officers assigned to these commands patrol the streets, respond to emergencies and to citizen calls for service, conduct preliminary investigations at crime scenes, investigate accidents, and enforce the city's traffic laws. Detective functions are the responsibility of the **Investigations Command**, which investigates crimes, locates and apprehends suspects, locates missing persons, and recovers stolen property. The Command is divided into a number of specialized divisions to investigate specific types of crimes such as homicide, robbery, auto theft, burglary and theft, vice, juvenile crimes, narcotics, and hate crimes.[3]

The **Information Services Command** is responsible for crime analysis, planning, and research; the department's record unit; and the computer services division. This Command is also responsible for applying for, and administering, government grants. The Emergency Communications Division of the Command is the department's dispatching center. It receives all calls for service, prioritizes them, and dispatches patrol officers to each call. The Command also includes the Inspections Division, which has among its duties the development of departmental standard operating procedures. Personnel matters are handled by the **Professional Development Command**, which is responsible for tasks such as recruitment, hiring, initial and in-service training, psychological services, and personnel development. The Police Chaplain is a member of this Command.[4]

The **Support Services Command** has a wide variety of functions. The Command's Identification Division operates a variety of laboratories (such as fingerprint, firearms, and voice imaging enhancement), as well as collecting and maintaining criminal history data on all suspects arrested for a crime that is at least a Class B misdemeanor. The Crime Lab Division is responsible for scientific analysis of evidence and for providing technical assistance to officers at major crime scenes. This division also includes a photographic laboratory. The Jail Division oversees the HPD jail, which houses all prisoners arrested by the HPD as well as some other local law enforcement agencies. The Command is also responsible for the management of department facilities and property, including all HPD vehicles. Many special situations, such as traffic accidents, the protection of local and visiting dignitaries, and security at special events, are handled by the **Tactical Support Command**. Other responsibilities of this Command include patrolling and responding to citizen calls for service in the city's Central Business District, participating in accident investigations, and recovering evidence and property from under water.[5]

Currently, the minimum entry requirements for the HPD include:

- be a U.S. citizen and have been a resident in the contiguous U.S. for a period of time that allows the department to conduct a comprehensive background check (exceptions may be made for members of the military serving overseas)

- be between the ages of 21 and 35 (individuals with at least five years active military service or law enforcement service have an age waiver up to the age of 45)

- have weight proportionate to height

- have at least 60 semester hours from an accredited college or university with a minimum 2.0 GPA or an honorable military discharge

- have a valid driver's license and proof of liability insurance

- have no felony or Class A misdemeanor convictions and no Class B misdemeanor convictions within the past ten years

- have no more than two moving violation convictions within the past 18 months

- stable credit history, family background, and employment background

- individuals with a prior military background must not have been convicted of any court-martial higher than a summary.[6]

The selection process takes between four and twelve months to complete and includes six separate phases. Applicants must successfully complete all phases to qualify for the police academy. The hiring process includes:

1. Register for and take a Civil Service Examination

2. Ranking, appointment and processing - applicants who have taken and passed the Civil Service Examination are contacted in order of their test ranking for processing, including completion of HPD application paperwork

3. Review of paperwork and documents and take the HPD Physical Agility Test. The Test includes a timed obstacle course as well as a timed set of push-ups and sit-ups

4. Undergo a polygraph examination, be fingerprinted and photographed by the HPD Identification Division, take the final interview, and review all paperwork

5. Undergo a background investigation

6. Medical and psychological examination, including a drug test

The department selects recruits based on civil service examination ranking and on completion and passing of all phases of the application process. Applicants enter the academy as positions become available and attend a 26-week academy training program, followed by time in the Officer Field Training Program. While in the academy, cadets are paid an annual salary of $26,024.70. Upon graduation and appointment as a probationary police officer, one's salary is increased to $28,169.18. The minimum salary for non-probationary officers is $31,439.72.[7]

The Dallas Police Department

The Dallas Police Department (DPD) is the second largest local police department in Texas. In 2002, the DPD employed a total of 2,846 sworn officers and 555 civilians.[8]

The department is divided into five bureaus. The **Patrol Bureau** is divided into six operational divisions. Each division is responsible for providing patrol services and conducting preliminary investigations within a geographic region. The **Investigations Bureau** is responsible for detective functions, and is divided into a number of specialized units and squads to investigate specific types of crimes. These include the Homicide Unit, Robbery Unit, Forgery Squad, Missing Persons Squad, Child Abuse Squad, and many others. The **Special Services Bureau** includes Internal Affairs, the department's Traffic Unit, and a Vehicle Crimes Squad. The **Support Services Bureau** is responsible for running support functions, such as the automobile pound and the property unit. Finally, the **Administrative Services Bureau** is responsible for recruiting and training new officers, and for providing services to DPD personnel. This Bureau runs the DPD Academy and provides both pre-service and in-service training.[9]

Currently, the minimum entry requirements for the DPD include:

- be a U.S. citizen
- have at least 45 semester hours from an accredited university or college with at least a "C" average
- be at least 21 years of age, or be 19.5 years of age and have at least 60 semester hours with at least a "C" average
- have no felony or Class A misdemeanor convictions
- meet departmental vision standards (no worse than 20/100 in either eye, correctable to 20/20 in both eyes, and normal color vision)
- have an honorable discharge from the military (if applicable)
- have a valid driver's license[10]

Applicants who meet these minimum criteria must then go through an eight-phase hiring process and successfully complete each phase. Failure at any stage will result in elimination from the selection pool. The phases include:

1. preliminary interview
2. civil service test
3. physical agility test
4. polygraph examination
5. applicant interview board
6. background investigation

7. psychological evaluation
8. medical evaluation[11]

Applicants who successfully complete the hiring process and receive appointments as Trainee Police Officers go through a 32-week training program at the Dallas Police Academy, where they study a wide variety of topics, including patrol procedures, vehicle operations, firearms and unarmed defense training, criminal law, investigation, and human relations. After graduation, officers serve a 24-week period with a field training officer. While attending the academy, trainees receive an annual base salary of $36,806. Trainees with a four-year college degree receive a higher base salary of $38,006. Upon graduation from the academy, trainee officers receive a lump sum bonus of $1,000.[12]

COUNTY POLICING

Each of the 254 counties in Texas has a separate **sheriff's department**. The Texas Constitution states that the sheriff of each county will be elected by the qualified voters of the county in a general election. All sheriffs serve terms of four years.[13] Therefore, partisan politics significantly influences county police agencies in the state. The Constitution requires that all sheriffs, deputy sheriffs, and other county law enforcement officers must be paid on a salary basis, rather than a fee basis.[14]

Most sheriff's departments in Texas are full-service police agencies that provide police services to all unincorporated areas of the county. In addition, incorporated towns or cities that do not wish to set up their own local police department may contract out to their county sheriff's department for police services. In most counties, there are no mandatory minimum training requirements which must be met by candidates running for sheriff. For example, candidates for sheriff are not required to have attended a police academy or to have any practical policing experience of any kind.

In many counties, the sheriff's department is not only responsible for providing law enforcement services to the county but also for running the county jail, maintaining security in all county courts, serving civil and criminal processes, and providing assistance when needed to local departments within the county. This assistance can range from operating a county-wide crime lab to assisting a local department with a criminal investigation. County sheriffs have police powers throughout the county, including within the boundaries of incorporated cities that maintain a city police force.

The Harris County Sheriff's Department

Harris County, TX, is located in southeast Texas and includes the city of Houston. It is one of the largest counties in the United States, with a population of over 3.4 million in 2000.[15] The **Harris County Sheriff's Department** (HCSD), which is one of the oldest law enforcement agencies in the state, was founded in 1837 with one mounted officer.[16] In 2002, the department had a total of 3,434 employees, of which 2,543 were sworn officers and 891 were civilians.[17]

The HCSD is divided into eight bureaus, each headed by an officer with the rank of major. The **Patrol Bureau** provides law enforcement services to unincorporated areas in Harris county. There are five patrol divisions. The **Central Patrol Division** includes traffic enforcement, the crime prevention unit, D.A.R.E., the department's mounted and marine patrols, and the Citizen's Police Academy. Deputies assigned to the patrol bureau are involved in criminal investigations, arrest offenders, enforce traffic laws, and investigate traffic accidents.[18]

The **Detective Bureau** is the criminal investigation unit of the HCSD. It is composed of 11 specialized divisions, including Crimes Against Persons, Crimes Against Property, Auto Theft, Criminal Warrants, the Organized Crime and Narcotics Task Force, Internal Affairs, and the Youth Violent Offender Unit, and the Youth Gang Intervention Unit. To be eligible for assignment to the detective bureau, a deputy must have been working for the HCSD for at least 18 months and pass the department's civil service examination for promotion to the rank of detective.

The department's **Technical Services Bureau** provides technical services to the HCSD. The Bureau's Communications Division handles all calls for service that come from unincorporated Harris County. The ID/AFIS Division is responsible for the Automated Fingerprint Identification System as well as for maintaining criminal history information on all offenders who are charged with at least a Class B misdemeanor in the county. The Systems Division deals with the development and maintenance of all computers and networks within the department. Finally, the Bureau's Alarm, Property, and Report's Division is responsible for regulating alarm use, storing and processing all found property and evidence, maintaining offense records of criminal incidents, and preparing the Harris County Uniform Crime Reports.

The **Human Resources Bureau** is responsible for training, personnel administration, inventory, payroll, bookkeeping, accreditation, and minority affairs. This bureau also runs the Harris County Sheriff's Academy. The **Support Services Bureau** and **Public Services Bureau** provide a variety of services to the department, including maintaining departmental vehicles, property and supply, internal affairs, and public information. The **Detention (701)** and **Detention (1301) Bureaus** refer to the two main inmate housing facilities in the Harris County Jail System.[19]

The El Paso County Sheriff's Office

El Paso county is located in western Texas. In 2002, the **El Paso County Sheriff's Office** (EPCSO) employed a total of 1,016 individuals, including 236 sworn deputies and 780 civilians.[20] The first sheriff of El Paso County, Sheriff William Ford, was appointed in 1852 when the county had a population of almost 1,000. Today, the EPCSO is responsible for serving over 600,000 county residents. The EPCSO is the first sheriff's office in the state to be nationally accredited by the Commission on Accreditation for Law Enforcement Agencies.[21]

The department is divided into five divisions. The **Patrol Division** includes uniformed patrol officers, school resource officers, a traffic section, an environmental crimes unit, and a drug interdiction unit. The **Criminal Investigations Division** provides detective services to the county. Duties include investigating crimes, arresting offenders, serving warrants, and assisting the prosecutor in preparing cases. The investigation of cases involving drug trafficking, drug organizations, and money laundering are the responsibility of the **Special Operations Division**. The **Detention Division** is responsible for housing individuals awaiting trial, inmates sentenced to a term of imprisonment in the county jail, federal offenders, individuals who are wanted in other jurisdictions, and convicted felony offenders awaiting transfer to a Texas Department of Corrections facility. Finally, the **Administration Division** provides support services to the EPCSO, including maintaining the department's motor vehicles, providing human resources services, and running the training academy.[22]

The Jefferson County Sheriff's Department

Jefferson County is located in southeast Texas. In 2002, the **Jefferson County Sheriff's Department** (JCSD) had a total of 403 employees, of which 97 were sworn officers and 306 were civilians.[23] The JCSD is divided into three main divisions. The **Law Enforcement Division** provides a wide range of law enforcement services to county residents. It includes patrol, criminal investigations, D.A.R.E., a street crimes unit, a S.W.A.T. team, auto theft and narcotics task forces, the department's communication division (which processes all calls for service), identification, and internal affairs. The Division's training unit runs the Sheriff's Peace Officer Academy, which serves all local law enforcement agencies within the county as well as JCSD law enforcement and correctional officers.[24]

The **Corrections Division** is responsible for running the Jefferson County Correctional Facility, a short-term facility housing both individuals awaiting trial and inmates sentenced to incarceration in a county facility. The Division also runs the Jefferson County Youth Academy (JCYA) Juvenile Justice Alternative Education Program (JJAEP) day boot camp. Participants range in age from 10 to 16, although a student who turns 17 while in the program may remain until s/he successfully completes program requirements. The program focuses on students at risk and on juvenile offenders who are on probation or deferred prosecution.

Finally, the **Services Division** provides a variety of special and support services to the Department. Special services include the Airborne Extradition Unit, the K-9 Unit, and the Aviation Unit (which operates helicopters to supplement ground patrol officers). The division is also responsible for support services, such as personnel, recruitment, maintenance and preservation of property and evidence, and for running the regional crime laboratory.[25]

STATE POLICING

There are two main types of **state police agencies** within the United States. Some states, such as North Carolina, separate or **decentralize** the functions and keep criminal investigations separate from the uniformed highway patrol. However, other states, including Texas operate a **centralized** or full-service state police agency which includes both highway patrol functions and criminal investigation.

The Texas Department of Public Safety

The **Texas Department of Public Safety** (DPS) was created as a statewide law enforcement agency in 1935 by the Texas Legislature. The new agency incorporated the Texas Highway Motor Patrol and the Texas Rangers.[26] According to the Government Code (GC) §411.002(a),

> The Department of Public Safety of the State of Texas is an agency of the state to enforce the laws protecting the public safety and provide for the prevention and detection of crime. The department is composed of the Texas Rangers, the Texas Highway Patrol, the administrative division, and other divisions that the commission considers necessary.

In 2002, the DPS had a total of 7,480 employees, of which 3,036 were sworn officers and 4,449 were civilians.[27]

Currently, the DPS is divided into six major divisions. The **Administration Division** is the staff support services arm of the DPS, providing administrative support to all other divisions within the Department. It maintains crime records and fingerprint files, operates the DPS Training Academy, is responsible for various personnel programs and functions, is in charge of the Department's fleet of vehicles, and provides a variety of other staff support functions. This division is also responsible for Texas emergency management services. The division's Uniform Crime Reporting (UCR) program collects data on crimes reported to or known to the police, provides data to the FBI's national UCR program, and publishes state crime statistics twice a year.[28]

The **Director's Staff**, which includes the Director of the DPS and two Assistant Directors, are responsible for overseeing all DPS functions. Several sections report directly to the director and assistant directors of the DPS, including Public Information, Accounting, Aircraft, Internal Affairs, Information Management, and General Counsel. The **Drivers License Division** issues and controls all drivers licenses in Texas. The Division was created in 1998 as a way of consolidating all the activities relating to drivers licenses throughout the state. Division responsibilities include testing new drivers, voter registration, and improvement and control of problem drivers.[29]

The **Criminal Law Enforcement Division** (CLE) was established in 1968 and focuses on law enforcement activities and provides specialized assistance not only to DPS officers but also to other law enforcement agencies throughout Texas. The Division is involved in a wide variety of multi-jurisdictional investigations, working with municipal, county, state, and federal agencies to combat crimes such as narcotics, motor vehicle theft, fraud, gambling, and public corruption. There are four specialized units or "services" within the CLE Division. The **Narcotics Service** is responsible for directing the statewide attempts to deter and eliminate illegal drug trafficking, supervising the registration of controlled substances, administering prescription requirements for certain controlled substances, and supervising the state's precursor chemical program (which controls chemicals that may be used in the illegal manufacture of drugs such as amphetamine and methamphetamine.) The **Motor Vehicle Theft Service** focuses specifically on motor vehicle theft in Texas, including control, deterrence, and vehicle recovery. In 2002, the state ranked second in the U.S. in auto theft offenses, with almost 103,000 vehicle theft losses. The **Special Crimes Service** gathers intelligence and information, investigates a variety of serious crimes, and administers a number of regulatory programs (e.g., sex offender registration). Currently the service, which is based in Austin, is focusing particularly on organized criminal groups. Finally, the **Crime Laboratory Service** provides forensic laboratory services and support to law enforcement agencies throughout Texas.[30]

In September, 2003, the **Traffic Law Enforcement Division** was renamed the **Texas Highway Patrol Division**. This Division is responsible for enforcing the law on Texas highways. The Division patrols rural highways in Texas, enforcing both traffic and criminal law. Current enforcement priorities include seat belt laws, speeding, drug violations, and intoxicated drivers, as well as other ongoing criminal activity. The Division's **Commercial Vehicle Enforcement Service** enforces laws that relate to commercial vehicles and commercial drivers licenses (such as the size, weight, and registration of commercial vehicles) as well as enforcing all traffic laws relating to commercial vehicles. The **Vehicle Inspection Service** is responsible for conducting emissions testing and general vehicle inspections of vehicles in Texas. Over 13 million vehicle inspections are performed each year. The **Communications Service** operates a statewide network serving the communications needs of criminal justice agencies throughout Texas. For example, police officers requesting driver's license status and vehicle registration information go through the DPS Communications Service. The service also is widely used by members of the public requesting police assistance. In 2002, the Service handled over 2 million telephone calls and over 11.5 million radio contacts. The Division is also responsible for the safety and security of Region VII, the Capitol Complex, a 46-square block area in downtown Austin with a daytime population of approximately 40,000 people. The Complex includes not only the State Capitol Building, but also 28 state office buildings, 27 garages and parking lots, and 15 private office buildings. The Capitol Detail protects the complex, assists visitors, controls traffic, supervises parking, and conducts investigations of any crimes occurring within the complex. The Detail also provides protection for visiting dignitaries as well as being responsible for security at the Texas Governor's Mansion.[31]

Finally, the **Texas Rangers Division** is one of the oldest law enforcement agencies in the U.S. and the oldest with statewide jurisdiction. The Texas Rangers focus primarily on the investigation of major felonies and other related crimes that are not the responsibility of other DPS Divisions. They deal primarily with crimes such as murder, rape, robbery, burglary, white collar crime, and government corruption. The Division has 140 members, including 118 sworn officers. In 2002, the

Rangers conducted a total of 5,307 investigations, resulting in 1,805 felony arrests and 199 misdemeanor arrests. They executed 293 search warrants, seized over $3.3 million in contraband, and recovered over $5.5 million in stolen property.[32]

The minimum standards that must be met by all individuals applying to the DPS include:

- must be at least 20 years of age upon appointment
- must be a U.S. citizen
- must have, or be eligible to obtain, a valid Texas driver license
- must pass a physical examination by a physician
- vision must be at least 20/200 uncorrected, with specified levels of correction by eyeglasses or contact lenses, and applicant must also meet other specified visual criteria
- must have at least 90 semester hours from an accredited university or college, although prior law enforcement or military experience may substitute for educational requirements
- must be of good moral character and habits – applicants with a final conviction for any felony, DWI, DUID, or misdemeanor domestic violence offense will be automatically disqualified
- must have a good traffic record

Applicants who receive an invitation to the DPS Training Academy are required to live at the Academy during the training period, which lasts for 26 weeks. After completing the Academy, trooper-trainees are required to pass a written licensing examination which is administered by the Texas Commission on Law Enforcement Officer Standards and Education. As of September 1, 2003, trooper-trainees received a salary of $2,516.66 per month while attending the DPS Academy. This was increased to $2,773.33 per month upon graduation and commission as a state trooper. Troopers who successfully complete the twelve-month probationary period receive a salary of 3,033.33 per month. Commissioned troopers may be assigned anywhere in the state.[33]

The Texas Public Safety Commission

The **Texas Public Safety Commission** is responsible for overseeing the DPS. According to GC 411.003, the Commission is composed of three members who are appointed by the governor and confirmed by the Senate. All members must be citizens of the state of Texas. They serve staggered six-year terms and receive no compensation for their service, although they may receive per diem for expenses. The chair of the Commission is appointed by the governor. The duties and powers of the commission are outlined in GC §411.004, which states that,

> The commission shall:
> (1) formulate plans and policies for:
> (A) enforcement of state criminal, traffic, and safety laws;
> (B) prevention of crime;

(C) detection and apprehension of persons who violate laws; and

(D) education of citizens of this state in the promotion of public safety and the observance of law;

(2) organize the department and supervise its operation;

(3) adopt rules considered necessary for carrying out the department's work;

(4) maintain records of all proceedings and official orders; and

(5) biennially submit a report of its work to the governor and legislature, including the commission's and director's recommendations.

POLICE TRAINING

Police departments today require highly qualified and well-trained officers. In Texas, the **Texas Commission on Law Enforcement Officer Standards and Education** (TCLEOSE), a state regulatory agency, establishes and maintains training standards for law enforcement and corrections officers in Texas. The Commission also develops training courses and monitors training programs throughout the state. TCLEOSE originally was established by GC §415, which was repealed in 1999. The agency is currently governed by Chapter 1701 of the Occupations Code (OC).

According to OC §1701.051, TCLEOSE consists of a total of nine members who are appointed by the governor with the advice and consent of the Senate. Of the nine members, three are law enforcement chief executive officers (e.g., a sheriff, constable, or chief of police), three are licensed officers with at least five years experience (at least two of whom are peace officers in non-supervisory positions with a law enforcement agency), and three are members of the general public. Members serve staggered six-year terms and receive no compensation for their service other than expenses. In addition, there are five *ex officio* members of the commission:

- the commissioner of higher education of the Texas Higher Education Coordinating Board
- the commissioner of the Texas Education Agency
- the director of the Department of Public Safety
- the executive director of the criminal justice division of the governor's office
- the attorney general of the state of Texas

According to Rule §217.1 of the Texas Administrative Code,[33] the minimum standards that must be met to receive a license as a peace officer, armed public security officer, or jailer in Texas include:

1. Minimum education requirement – be a high school graduate, pass the GED, or have 12 semester hours of credit from an accredited college or university

2. Minimum age requirement – applicants must be at least 21 years of age, or 18 years of age if they received an associate's degree or 60 semester hours of credit from an accredited college or university or an honorable discharge after at least two years of active service with the U.S. armed forces. Applicants for the position of jailor must be at least 18 years of age.

3. Undergo fingerprinting and a check of local, state, and national records to discover any criminal record

4. Never have been placed on probation or court-ordered community supervision for any crime above the level of Class B misdemeanor, or for any Class B misdemeanor within the last ten years

5. Not be currently under indictment for any criminal offense

6. Never have been convicted of any crime above the level of Class B misdemeanor, or of any Class B misdemeanor within the last ten years

7. Never have been convicted at any time of any family violence offense

8. May not be prohibited by state or federal law from operating a motor vehicle

9. May not be prohibited by state or federal law from possession of a firearm or ammunition

10. Must undergo a background investigation and interview prior to appointment

11. Must undergo a medical examination by a licensed physician within 180 days of appointment and be found to be physically sound, free of any defect that might adversely affect the performance of required duties, and have no trace of illegal drug use or drug dependency

12. Must undergo an examination by a licensed psychologist within 180 days of appointment and be found to be in satisfactory emotional and psychological health

13. May not have received a less-than-honorable discharge from any military service, including a bad conduct or dishonorable discharge

14. May not have had a license denied by final order or revoked, may not currently be on suspension for a criminal violation, and may not have a voluntary surrender of license currently in effect

15. Must meet all minimum training standards and pass the commission licensing examination

16. May not violate any rules or provisions of OC §1701

The individual must also successfully complete all minimum training that is required for the license.

TCLEOSE develops and maintains courses for preparatory training and continuing education of police officers, county jailers, and emergency telecommunications operators. Potential officers and jailers are required to take a licensing examination. The commission also regulates minimum requirements for police officer pre-service and in-service training. In January, 2002, the minimum length of the basic peace officer course was increased to 576 hours. Individual departments are free to require a longer period of training. After pre-service training is successfully completed, all candidates must pass a state licensing examination, which is developed and administered by the Commission. Candidates passing this examination receive a peace officer license. Jailer candidates are also required to pass a similar examination.[34]

In-service training or education is that which an individual receives after employment and performing the duties of that position. In police work, in-service training is conducted after the individual has some policing experience and continues throughout the officer's career. The purpose of in-service training is to ensure that all officers are kept informed of current legislative statutes, department regulations, and community expectations of the organization.

According to Rule §217.11 of the Texas Administrative Code, all police officers are required to attend a minimum of 40 hours of in-service training every two years, although agencies are not limited to this minimum number of hours of continuing education and most officers in Texas receive more than the minimum required amount of training. Today, many in-service classes are offered over the Internet. Mandatory topics required of all officers include:

- training in civil rights, racial sensitivity, and cultural diversity

- training in recognition and documentation of cases involving child abuse, child neglect, family violence, sexual assault, and issues concerning sex offender characteristics

- supervisory training for any officer appointed to his or her first supervisory position – this must be completed within 24 months of the date of appointment as a supervisor.

Other requirements are specified by the Code for constables, deputy constables, and supervisory peace officers. An officer who fails to complete the required in-service/continuing education training may have his or her license suspended by the Commission.

NOTES

1. Houston Police Department web site (http://www.ci.houston.tx.us/departme/police/home.htm)
2. *Uniform Crime Reports* (http://www.fbi.gov/ucr/ucr.htm)
3. Houston Police Department web site, *op cit.*
4. *Ibid*
5. *Ibid*
6. *Ibid*
7. *Ibid*
8. *Uniform Crime Reports, op cit.*
9. Dallas Police Department web site (http://www.dallaspolice.net/)
10. *Ibid*
11. *Ibid*
12. *Ibid*
13. Texas State Constitution, Article 5, Section 23
14. Texas State Constitution, Article 16, Section 61
15. U.S. Census Bureau (http://www.census.gov)
16. Harris County Sheriff's Department web site (http://www.co.harris.tx.us/so/)
17. *Uniform Crime Reports, op cit.*
18. Harris County Sheriff's Department web site, *op cit.*
19. *Ibid*
20. *Uniform Crime Reports, op cit.*
21. El Paso County Sheriff's Office web site (http://www.co.el-paso.tx.us/sheriff/index.htm)
22. *Ibid*
23. *Uniform Crime Reports, op cit.*
24. Jefferson County Sheriff's Department home page (http://co.jefferson.tx.us/sheriff/mission.htm)
25. *Ibid*
26. Texas Department of Public Safety home page (http://www.txdps.state.tx.us/)
27. *Uniform Crime Reports, op cit.*
28. Texas Department of Public Safety home page, *op cit.*
29. *Ibid*
30. *Ibid*
31. *Ibid*

32. *Ibid*

33. See Texas Administrative Code, Title 317, Part 7, Chapter 217

34. Texas Commission on Law Enforcement home page (http://www.tcleose.state.tx.us/index.htm)

CHAPTER 5

THE COURT SYSTEM IN TEXAS

The Texas court system, which includes the criminal courts, is somewhat more complex than the court system found in most other states. Texas' court structure has five levels, including two top-level appellate courts, an intermediate appellate court, state trial courts of general jurisdiction, county trial courts of limited jurisdiction, and local trial courts of limited jurisdiction.[1]

UNITED STATES FEDERAL COURTS

There are a number of federal courts which sit in Texas. These are not part of the Texas state court system and should not be confused with the state trial and appellate courts.

There are four **U.S. District Courts** which sit in Texas.[2] These are the trial courts of the federal system. These courts include the Northern District Court, with 12 authorized active judgeships; the Southern District Court, with 18 authorized judgeships; the Western District Court, with 12 authorized judgeships; and the Eastern District Court, with 14 authorized judgeships.

The **U.S. Courts of Appeals** are the intermediate appellate courts of the federal court system and have appellate jurisdiction only over federal laws. Judges in these courts are nominated by the President of the United States and confirmed by the Senate. They serve life terms. Texas, along with Louisiana and Mississippi, is part of the Fifth Circuit, which sits in New Orleans, LA.[3] The U.S. Courts of Appeals should not be confused with the Texas Courts of Appeals, which are part of the Texas state court system, and are discussed below.

THE BASIC COURT STRUCTURE OF TEXAS

According to Article 5, Section 1 of the Texas Constitution,

> The judicial power of this State shall be vested in one Supreme Court, in one Court of Criminal Appeals, in Courts of Appeals, in District Courts, in County Courts, in Commissioners Courts, in Courts of Justices of the Peace, and in such other courts as may be provided by law...

Texas has a five-tier court structure. Unlike most states, which have one "court of last resort", Texas has two. The two top-level appellate courts in Texas are the Texas Supreme Court and the Texas Court of Criminal Appeals. These courts are of equal rank but have different jurisdictions. Together, they serve as the highest appellate courts in the state. The second level includes the Courts of Appeals, which serve as the intermediate appellate courts for the state of Texas.

The lower levels of the court structure include trial courts of general or limited jurisdiction. The third level is composed of state trial courts of general jurisdiction. In Texas, these are known as District Courts, and should not to be confused with the U.S. District Courts discussed above. The fourth tier includes county trial courts of limited jurisdiction. All counties have a Constitutional County Court. In addition, some counties also have County Courts at Law and/or Statutory Probate Courts. These courts are of equal rank but differ in their jurisdictions. Finally, the fifth tier includes local trial courts of limited jurisdiction. These include Municipal Courts and Justice of the Peace Courts.

Not all of these courts have criminal jurisdiction. According to Article 4.01 of the Code of Criminal Procedure (CCrP):

> The following courts have jurisdiction in criminal actions:
> 1. The Court of Criminal Appeals;
> 2. Courts of appeals;
> 3. The district courts;
> 4. The criminal district courts;
> 5. The magistrates appointed by the judges of the district courts of Bexar County, Dallas County, Tarrant County, or Travis County that give preference to criminal cases and the magistrates appointed by the judges of the criminal district courts of Dallas County or Tarrant County;
> 6. The county courts;
> 7. All county courts at law with criminal jurisdiction;
> 8. County criminal courts;
> 9. Justice courts;
> 10. Municipal courts; and
> 11. The magistrates appointed by the judges of the district courts of Lubbock County.

TEXAS' HIGHEST APPELLATE COURTS

As noted above, Texas has two high-level appellate courts authorized to hear final appeals: the Texas Supreme Court and the Texas Court of Criminal Appeals.

The Supreme Court of Texas

The **Texas Supreme Court** has final appellate jurisdiction in all civil and juvenile cases throughout Texas. It has no criminal jurisdiction. The Supreme Court generally hears cases on appeal from one of the intermediate Courts of Appeals. The Court is composed of a total of nine justices, including a Chief Justice. Five justices constitute a quorum and the concurrence of at least five of the nine justices is required to decide a case. To be eligible to serve as a Supreme Court justice, an individual must be at least 35 years of age, be a citizen of both the United States and of Texas, be licensed to practice law in Texas, and have been a practicing lawyer, or a lawyer and judge of a court of record, for at least ten years. Justices are elected to six-year terms at a general election.[4]

The Court of Criminal Appeals

The **Court of Criminal Appeals** has final appellate jurisdiction in the state over all appeals that result from criminal cases. Most cases are appeals from the Courts of Appeals, the intermediate appellate courts in Texas. Cases may be appealed to the Court of Criminal Appeals by petition for discretionary review which can be filed by the state and/or the defendant. In addition, all cases that involve a sentence of death are automatically appealed directly to the Court of Criminal Appeals from the trial court level. The court also has the right to review any decision on its own motion. The jurisdiction of the Court of Criminal Appeals is outlined in CCrP 4.04, which states that:

> Sec. 1. The Court of Criminal Appeals and each judge thereof shall have, and is hereby given, the power and authority to grant and issue and cause the issuance of writs of habeas corpus, and, in criminal law matters, the writs of mandamus, procedendo, prohibition, and certiorari. The court and each judge thereof shall have, and is hereby given, the power and authority to grant and issue and cause the issuance of such other writs as may be necessary to protect its jurisdiction or enforce its judgments.
>
> Sec. 2. The Court of Criminal Appeals shall have, and is hereby given, final appellate and review jurisdiction in criminal cases coextensive with the limits of the state, and its determinations shall be final. The appeal of all cases in which the death penalty has been assessed shall be to the Court of Criminal Appeals. In addition, the Court of Criminal Appeals may, on its own motion, with or without a petition for such discretionary review being filed by one of the parties, review any decision of a court of appeals in a criminal case. Discretionary review by the Court of Criminal Appeals is not a matter of right, but of sound judicial discretion.

The Court of Criminal Appeals sits in Austin and is made up of nine judges, one of whom serves as the Presiding Judge. The qualifications needed to serve as a judge in the Court of Criminal Appeals are the same as those required for Supreme Court Justices, and Court of Criminal Appeals judges receive the same salaries as their counterparts in the Supreme Court. All judges are elected to six-year terms. The court may sit in panels of three judges to hear cases. In cases involving a three-judge panel, two judges constitute a quorum and the agreement of two judges is required for a decision. For any proceedings involving capital punishment, the full court must convene. In these situations, five judges constitute a quorum and the agreement of five judges is required for a decision.[5]

During FY 2001-2002, the Court of Criminal Appeals disposed of 438 direct appeals. A total of 1,951 petitions for discretionary review were filed and 146 of these were granted by the Court.[6]

TEXAS COURTS OF APPEALS

The intermediate appellate courts in Texas are known as **Courts of Appeals**. One Court of Appeals is located in each of the fourteen appellate districts in the state. The specific counties falling into each of the districts is outlined in Section 22.201 of the Government Code (GC). These courts have intermediate appellate jurisdiction within their districts in both civil and criminal cases that have been appealed from either district courts or county-level courts, except for those cases which involved a sentence of death.

Each Court of Appeals has a Chief Justice and at least two, but not more than twelve, additional justices. All justices must meet the same qualifications required of Supreme Court justices and Court of Criminal Appeals judges. The exact number of judges assigned to each Court of Appeals is determined by statute and listed in GC §22.216. The largest is the Court of Appeals for the Fifth District, which consists of a chief justice and twelve justices. This district is composed of seven counties: Collin, Dallas, Grayson, Hunt, Kaufman, Rockwall, and Van Zandt; the court sits primarily in the City of Dallas. Currently, there are a total of 80 justices authorized to sit in the 14 Courts of Appeals. Most appeals in these courts are heard by a panel of three judges, with the agreement of a majority of the judges sitting required to decide a case.[7]

During FY 2001-2002, the Courts of Appeals disposed of 6,995 criminal cases and 5,404 civil cases.[8]

TEXAS DISTRICT COURTS

Texas District Courts serve as the state's trial courts of general jurisdiction. The state is divided into judicial districts, each of which has a district court with one or more judges. District judges are elected to four-year terms. To qualify as a district judge, a candidate must be a citizen of the United States and of Texas, must be at least 25 years of age, must be licensed to practice law in Texas, must have been a practicing lawyer or judge in a Texas court for at least four years prior to his or her election to district judge, and must have resided in the district from which s/he is elected for at least two years preceding the election. All district court judges are required to live in their districts during their terms of office.[9]

The area served by each district is established by the state legislature. Each county must have at least one district court. In some of the less populated areas of the state, a single district court may serve several counties. On the other hand, some very highly populated urban counties may be served by multiple district courts. As of September 1, 2002, there were a total of 418 district courts in Texas. These courts disposed of a total of 218,097 criminal cases, 492,061 civil cases, and 36,482 juvenile cases.[10]

The jurisdiction of the district court is outlined in Article V, Section 8, of the Texas Constitution, which states that:

> District Court jurisdiction consists of exclusive, appellate, and original jurisdiction of all actions, proceedings, and remedies, except in cases where exclusive, appellate, or original jurisdiction may be conferred by this Constitution or other law on some other court, tribunal, or administrative body. District Court judges shall have the power to issue writs necessary to enforce their jurisdiction. The District Court shall have appellate jurisdiction and general supervisory control over the County Commissioners Court, with such exceptions and under such regulations as may be prescribed by law.

Essentially, district courts have original jurisdiction over all felony criminal cases, all civil cases involving at least $200, all divorce cases, and various other matters. Most district courts handle both civil and criminal cases but some district courts, located in more highly-populated counties, may specialize in criminal, civil, family law, or juvenile cases.

COUNTY TRIAL COURTS OF LIMITED JURISDICTION

The fourth level of courts in Texas is the **County Trial Courts of Limited Jurisdiction**. There are three different types of county courts. All counties must have a Constitutional County Courts. In addition, some counties may also have County Courts at Law and/or Statutory Probate Courts.

Constitutional County Courts

According to the Texas Constitution, each of the 254 counties in Texas is required to have a **Constitutional County Court**.[11] The presiding officer of the court, the county judge, is elected by voters in the county to a four-year term. To be a county judge, an individual must be "well informed in the law of the State [and] a conservator of the peace..."[12] Each county is specifically limited to only one county court.

Constitutional County Courts have limited civil and criminal jurisdiction. They generally hear probate cases filed in the county (unless the county has a Statutory Probate Court), have original jurisdiction over all Class A and Class B misdemeanor cases, and, in those counties which have not established County Courts at Law, have appellate jurisdiction over those cases which are appealed from municipal courts or justice of the peace courts. Unless the appeal is being made from a municipal court of record, the appeal consists of a completely new trial, which is known as a ***trial de novo***.[13]

County Courts at Law

Each county in Texas is constitutionally limited to only one county court. However, in some of the larger counties in the state, this single court has become unable to handle the large number of cases. As a result, the state legislature created statutory county courts, known as **County Courts at Law**, to assist the county court. County courts at law are trial courts. Their jurisdiction varies by county and is determined by the statute that created each specific court. In most counties, these courts have appellate jurisdiction over cases appealed from justice of the peace or municipal courts.[14]

Statutory Probate Courts

In most counties, the Constitutional County Court has original probate jurisdiction. However, in some counties the state legislature has authorized the creation of **Statutory Probate Courts**. The six largest metropolitan areas in the state have Statutory Probate Courts, which have original jurisdiction over probate matters, guardianship issues, and mental health commitments within the county. In addition, in some counties, statutory probate courts and the constitutional county court have concurrent jurisdiction over probate matters.[15]

LOCAL TRIAL COURTS OF LIMITED JURISDICTION

The fifth and lowest level of courts in Texas are the **Local Trial Courts of Limited Jurisdiction**. There are two main types of courts that fall into this category: Municipal Courts and Justice of the Peace Courts.

Municipal Courts

According to GC §29.002, each municipality in Texas shall have a **Municipal Court**. As of September 1, 2002, there were municipal courts in 877 incorporated cities and towns in Texas. Larger cities may have multiple municipal courts, depending on the city's population and individual needs.[16]

The jurisdiction of the Municipal Court is outlined in CCrP 4.14, which states that:

> (a) A municipal court, including a municipal court of record, shall have exclusive original jurisdiction within the municipality's territorial limits and property owned by the municipality located in the municipality's extraterritorial jurisdiction in all criminal cases that:
> (1) arise under the ordinances of the municipality; and
> (2) are punishable by a fine not to exceed:
> (A) $2,000 in all cases arising under municipal ordinances or resolutions, rules, or orders of a joint board that govern fire safety, zoning, or public health and sanitation, including dumping of refuse; or
> (B) $500 in all other cases arising under a municipal ordinance.
>
> (b) The municipal court has concurrent jurisdiction with the justice court of a precinct in which the municipality is located in all criminal cases arising under state law that:

(1) arise within the territorial limits of the municipality and are punishable only by a fine, as defined in Subsection (c) of this article; or

(2) arise under Chapter 106, Alcoholic Beverage Code, and do not include confinement as an authorized sanction.

(c) In this section, an offense which is punishable by "fine only" is defined as an offense that is punishable by fine and such sanctions, if any, as authorized by statute not consisting of confinement in jail or imprisonment.

(d) The fact that a conviction in a municipal court has as a consequence the imposition of a penalty or sanction by an agency or entity other than the court, such as a denial, suspension, or revocation of a privilege, does not affect the original jurisdiction of the municipal court.

(e) The municipal court has jurisdiction in the forfeiture and final judgment of all bail bonds and personal bonds taken in criminal cases of which the court has jurisdiction.

Essentially, Municipal Courts have original jurisdiction over all violations of city ordinances and have concurrent jurisdiction with justice of the peace courts over any Class C misdemeanors that are only punishable by a fine. They generally do not have jurisdiction in civil cases, with the exception of cases involving owners of dangerous dogs. Municipal judges have the power to issue search warrants and arrest warrants.[17]

Justice of the Peace Courts

Each county is required by the Constitution to establish between one and eight justice of the peace precincts. The actual number of precincts in each county is determined by the county population.[18] Each precinct has either one or two **Justice of the Peace Courts**, depending on the population of the precinct. During FY 2001-2002, there were 834 justice of the peace courts operating in Texas, each with at least one justice of the peace presiding.[19] Justices of the peace are elected by the voters of the precinct to four-year terms.

Justice of the Peace Courts have original jurisdiction over minor civil cases and over Class C misdemeanor criminal cases. They also serve as a small claims court. Justices of the peace have the power to issue search warrants and arrest warrants, and also serve as the county coroner if the county does not provide for a medical examiner.[20]

OTHER COURT AGENCIES AND COMMISSIONS

The Texas Office of Court Administration

The **Texas Office of Court Administration** (OCA) provides technical assistance and administrative support to courts throughout the state. The OCA operates under the direction of the chief justice of the Texas Supreme Court.[21]

The duties and responsibilities of the OCA include providing software to assist the courts in tracking caseloads and automating reports; providing technical support to courts; and supplying information on recent developments and court trends to the legislature, the courts, and members of the general public. The OCA is also responsible for gathering official statistics from court officials throughout the state.[22]

The State Commission on Judicial Conduct

The **State Commission on Judicial Conduct** was created in 1965 by the passage of Article 5, Section 1-a, of the Texas Constitution and is responsible for reviewing all complaints regarding misconduct or disability of judges and justices in Texas. The commission has jurisdiction over all judicial officers in the state. Currently, there are over 3,500 judicial officers under the jurisdiction of the commission.[23]

The Commission has a total of eleven members. It includes five judges, one from a court of appeals, one from a district court, one justice of the peace, one municipal court judge, and one county court at law judge. There are also four members who are members of the State Bar of Texas, who are not judges and who have practiced law for at least ten consecutive years prior to their selection, and four citizen members who are at least 30 years of age and who are not judges or attorneys.[24]

After receiving a complaint about a judge or justice, the commission investigates and then holds a hearing. If the commission determines that the judge or justice is guilty of some type of misconduct that is inconsistent with the proper performance of his or her duties, the commission may:

- privately reprimand the judge
- publicly censure the judge
- impose an order of education (generally in cases where the judge exceeded his or her authority or violated procedural rules)
- suspend the judge with or without pay
- recommend to the Texas Supreme Court that the judge be removed or retired.[25]

The State Bar of Texas

In 1939, the state legislature passed the **State Bar Act**, which required all attorneys who are licensed to practice law in Texas to be members of the State Bar. The **State Bar of Texas** is an administrative agency under the authority of the judicial branch of the state government. It is a public corporation funded by attorney dues and Professional Development Program Fees and is responsible for providing educational programs for the legal profession and the public, administering the Minimum Continuing Legal Education program for attorneys, and managing the lawyer disciplinary process.[26]

TEXAS CRIMINAL COURT PROCEDURES

The basic procedures involved in a criminal trial, including the pretrial activities, are similar in most states. In Texas, the process begins when the police are notified (or in some other way discover) that a crime has been committed and they initiate an investigation into that crime. The procedures discussed in this section apply to felony offenses. However, the procedures for misdemeanors are extremely similar.

Arrest and Booking

After the police have determined both that a crime has in fact been committed and that a specific person committed the crime, they may place that individual under **arrest**. In some situations, the police may have obtained an **arrest warrant** from a judge. An arrest warrant is,

> a written order from a magistrate, directed to a peace officer or some other person specially named, commanding him to take the body of the person accused of an offense, to be dealt with according to law.[27]

Chapter 15 of the Code of Criminal Procedure discusses the legal issues relating to arrests made under warrant. However, in Texas, the vast majority of arrests are made by police officers acting without a warrant. Chapter 14 of the Code of Criminal Procedure discusses situations in which it is lawful to make an arrest without a warrant.

After a suspect has been arrested and taken to the county jail, s/he goes through the **booking** procedure, which involves entering into the police record various facts about the suspect. At this time, the suspect will be photographed and fingerprinted and may be placed in a police lineup.

Initial Appearance

Within 24 hours of arrest, the defendant must be brought before a judge for an **initial appearance**. At this time, the judge will inform the defendant of the charges being brought against him or her and will determine whether the defendant is entitled to any form of **pretrial release**, including **bail**. Although the U.S. Supreme Court stated in *Stack v. Boyle*[28] that the U.S. Constitution does not guarantee the right to bail, the Texas State Constitution does provide a substantive right to bail, except in capital cases.[29] The court has a number of options when considering pretrial release. These include:

- requiring a payment of cash bail in exchange for pretrial release
- requiring a payment of non-cash bail – usually a property bond where the defendant deposits some form of property as collateral for release

- allowing release on personal recognizance – where the defendant is released without any bail

- conditional release – where the defendant is required as a condition of pretrial release to attend a treatment or other type of program or to remain under the supervision of a specific individual or agency

The prosecution may charge the defendant either by an **information** or by a **grand jury indictment**. Both are formal written charging instruments that specify the identity of the accused individual, the specific crime alleged to have been committed, and the court which has jurisdiction to try the case. An information is "a written statement filed and presented in behalf of the State by the district or county attorney, charging the defendant with an offense which may by law be so prosecuted."[30] A grand jury indictment is "the written statement of a grand jury accusing a person therein named of some act or omission which, by law, is declared to be an offense."[31] Capital felonies may only be charged by indictment.

Grand juries are organized by the district judge and have jurisdiction only over those crimes occurring within the county. They generally have 12 jurors. A grand jury is not responsible for determining the guilt or innocence of the defendant. Its purpose is simply to decide whether or not there is sufficient evidence to charge the individual with a crime. For an indictment or **true bill** to be issued, at least nine of the twelve grand jurors must agree. If the grand jury does not find that there is sufficient evidence to charge the suspect, the case is **no billed** and the suspect is immediately discharged. A finding of no bill does not prevent this or any other grand jury from indicting the same suspect at a later data.

Arraignment

The next stage in the criminal process is the **arraignment**. According to CCrP 26.01:

> In all felony cases, after indictment, and all misdemeanor cases punishable by imprisonment, there shall be an arraignment.

At this time, the defendant is asked to plead to the charges. S/he may plead guilty or not guilty. Some judges, but not all, will also permit a plea of ***nolo contendere***. A plea of *nolo contendere* has the same legal effect as a plea of guilty.[32] This plea is not very common. In most cases, defendants will plead either guilty or not guilty. If the accused pleads guilty (or *nolo contendere*), there is no need for the case to go to trial and the offender will be sentenced.

If the defendant has been charged with a felony or a misdemeanor that is punishable by imprisonment and cannot afford to hire an attorney, the court at this time will appoint an attorney to represent the defendant. Court-appointed attorneys are not appointed for indigent defendants in cases where the defendant is charged with a crime that will not result in a possible term of imprisonment.

Plea Bargaining

While plea bargaining is not a formal stage of the criminal justice process, it is an extremely important element in every state, including Texas. The majority of all felony and misdemeanor convictions in Texas are the result of guilty pleas. Only a small percentage of criminal cases actually go to trial. Generally, plea bargaining involves an attempt to resolve or dispose of a case without a trial, by an agreement between the prosecutor and the defendant, made under judicial supervision.

During this process, the prosecutor negotiates with the defense attorney (or the defendant). The purpose of the negotiation is to reach an agreement whereby the defendant will enter a plea of guilty (or *nolo contendere*) to a charge. In some plea agreements the prosecutor allows the defendant to plead guilty to a less serious offense than the one with which the defendant was originally charged. This type of plea bargain reduces the range of possible sentences that the judge may impose. In other cases, the plea of guilty is made in exchange for some action on the part of the prosecutor, which may include one or more of the following:

- drop other charges which have been filed against the defendant
- make recommendations to the court concerning sentencing
- agree not to oppose the defendant's request for a certain sentence
- agree to a specific sentence

The defense attorney is responsible for advising the defendant of all plea offers and any other relevant matters that may affect the defendant's decision, such as the possible results of each plea. The defense attorney may not accept any plea bargain without the full consent of the defendant. Although the trial judge does not participate directly in plea bargaining, s/he is still an important element in the process because all plea agreements must be approved by the judge. Plea bargaining often begins at the arraignment stage but may continue up to and even during the trial.

Pre-Trial Motions

Prior to the trial, both the defense and the prosecution have the opportunity to make a variety of **pre-trial motions**. A **motion for continuance** is a request that the trial be delayed for a period of time and may be made by either the prosecution or the defense.[33] A **motion for a change of venue** may be filed by either the prosecution or the defendant. This motion requests that the location of the trial be changed on the grounds that it is not possible to obtain a fair and impartial trial in the county where the case is currently pending.[34] A **motion to suppress evidence** considers whether evidence to be presented at trial was obtained illegally (e.g., through an unlawful search and seizure) and should therefore be prohibited from use as evidence in court.[35] A **motion to dismiss** is filed by the defense and claims that there are no grounds for bringing the defendant to trial.

The Right to a Speedy Trial

The Texas Constitution provides for the right to a speedy trial.[36] In Texas, each case must be brought to trial within a certain specified period of time, which is outlined in CCrP 32A.02, Section 1:

> A court shall grant a motion to set aside an indictment, information, or complaint if the state is not ready for trial within:
> (1) 180 days of the commencement of a criminal action if the defendant is accused of a felony;
> (2) 90 days of the commencement of a criminal action if the defendant is accused of a misdemeanor punishable by a sentence of imprisonment for more than 180 days; or
> (3) 60 days of the commencement of a criminal action if the defendant is accused of a misdemeanor punishable by a sentence of imprisonment for 180 days or less or punishable by a fine only.

Any delays in brining the case to trial that are due to actions or proceedings that involve the defendant are not included in the specified maximum pre-trial period.[37] If the prosecutor is not ready to try the case within the legally specified period, and the defendant is not responsible for the delay, the judge, upon a motion by the defense, must dismiss the case. If the defendant fails to move for dismissal under the provisions of the statute prior to the start of the trial, the defendant has waived his or her rights under the statute.[38]

The Trial

The majority of felony and misdemeanor cases are disposed of by a plea of guilty on the part of the defendant. Only a small percentage go to a formal criminal **trial**. If the defendant enters a plea of not guilty and the case does go to trial, the procedure is similar regardless of the seriousness of the charge against the defendant.

All defendants are constitutionally guaranteed the right to a **trial by jury.**[39] However, with the consent of the judge and the prosecutor, a defendant may waive the right to a jury trial and be tried in front of a judge. This is known as a **bench trial**. A defendant charged with a capital felony in which the state plans to seek the death penalty may not waive his or her right to a trial by jury. The order of proceeding in a trial by jury in Texas is specified in CCrP 36.01.

Jury Selection

The first step in a trial is the **selection of the jury**. District court juries are composed of twelve jurors while county courts and justice of the peace courts use six-person juries.[40] The process of jury selection is known as ***voir dire*** and involves an examination of the prospective jurors by the court and by the attorneys for both the prosecution and the defense. The main purpose of the *voir dire* is to determine whether each potential juror is impartial and will be able to render a fair verdict in a case. Potential jurors are placed under oath and then questioned by the judge, prosecutor, and defense counsel.

During the *voir dire* process, both the defense and the prosecutor are allowed to make challenges, which involve objecting to the inclusion of certain individuals in the trial jury. Like most states, Texas allows two specific types of challenges. A **challenge for cause** is made when the attorney feels that for some reason the juror is unfit or incapable of serving on the jury. Challenges for cause may be made by either the prosecution or the defense for any of the following reasons:

1. That he is not a qualified voter in the state and county under the Constitution and laws of the state; provided, however, the failure to register to vote shall not be a disqualification;
2. That he has been convicted of theft or any felony;
3. That he is under indictment or other legal accusation for theft or any felony;
4. That he is insane;
5. That he has such defect in the organs of feeling or hearing, or such bodily or mental defect or disease as to render him unfit for jury service, or that he is legally blind and the court in its discretion is not satisfied that he is fit for jury service in that particular case;
6. That he is a witness in the case;
7. That he served on the grand jury which found the indictment;
8. That he served on a petit jury in a former trial of the same case;
9. That he has a bias or prejudice in favor of or against the defendant;
10. That from hearsay, or otherwise, there is established in the mind of the juror such a conclusion as to the guilt or innocence of the defendant as would influence him in his action in finding a verdict...
11. That he cannot read or write.[41]

In addition, there are several types of challenges for cause that may only be made by the prosecution. These challenges may be made for any of the following reasons:

1. That the juror has conscientious scruples in regard to the infliction of the punishment of death for crime, in a capital case, where the State is seeking the death penalty;
2. That he is related within the third degree of consanguinity or affinity... to the defendant; and
3. That he has a bias or prejudice against any phase of the law upon which the State is entitled to rely for conviction or punishment.[42]

There are also several challenges for cause that may only be made by the defense. According to CCrP §35.16(c), the defense (but not the prosecution) may challenge a potential juror for cause on the following grounds:

1. That he is related within the third degree of consanguinity or affinity ... to the person injured by the commission of the offense, or to any prosecutor in the case; and
2. That he has a bias or prejudice against any of the law applicable to the case upon which the defense is entitled to rely, either as a defense to some phase of the offense for which the defendant is being prosecuted or as a mitigation thereof or of the punishment therefor.

Peremptory challenges may be used by either attorney to remove potential jurors from the jury panel without giving any specific reasons.[43] The number of peremptory challenges allowed each attorney is determined by the seriousness of the case. In a capital case where the death penalty is being sought, both the defense and the prosecution are allowed fifteen peremptory challenges. In non-capital felony cases and in capital cases where the death penalty is not being sought, each side is allowed ten peremptory challenges. In misdemeanor cases tried in district court, five peremptory challenges are allowed; if the case is being tried in the county court or county court at law, three are permitted.[44] Although no reason has to be assigned to a peremptory challenge, peremptory challenges based on the race of the prospective juror are specifically prohibited.[45]

After the selection of the jury is completed, the jurors are sworn in by the court and seated in the jury box. The oath of trial jurors in Texas is:

> "You and each of you do solemnly swear that in the case of the State of Texas against the defendant, you will a true verdict render according to the law and the evidence, so help you God".[46]

The information or indictment is read to the jury by the prosecutor and the defendant enters a formal plea before the court.

Opening Statements

Both the prosecutor and the defense attorney are entitled to make an **opening statement** which provides all the participants in the trial, especially the jury, with an overview of the facts of the case. In Texas, the prosecutor makes the first statement. After the prosecution's opening remarks are completed, the defense may make an opening statement immediately or may choose to wait until the start of the defense case.

Presentation of the Prosecution's Evidence

After the opening statements are completed, the prosecution begins to present evidence in support of the charge that has been brought against the defendant. The prosecution presents first because the state is bringing the charge against the defendant and, because of the presumption of innocence, has assumed the burden of proof. In Texas, evidence submitted into court may include the sworn testimony of witnesses as well as exhibits such as pictures, documents, recordings, depositions, or other objects.

The prosecutor generally begins with the **direct examination** of the prosecution's first witness, who is obviously expected to give evidence to support the state's case against the defendant. After the prosecutor finishes questioning the witness, the defense is allowed to **cross-examine** the same witness. If the prosecutor wishes, s/he may then return to ask the witness more questions in a process that is known as **re-direct examination**. Following this, the defense attorney has the option to question the witness once more during the **re-cross examination**. This procedure is repeated for each witness called by the prosecution.

Presentation of the Defense's Evidence

After the prosecution has presented all its evidence and called all its witnesses, the defense is given the option of offering evidence. Although the prosecution is required to present evidence in support of the indictment, the presentation of evidence in defense of the defendant is optional. If the defense attorney chose not to make an opening statement at the start of the trial, s/he may make one now. The procedure for the presentation of the evidence by the defense is similar to that of the prosecution: direct examination, cross examination, re-direct, and re-cross. The defendant is not required to testify at any point in the trial; both the U.S. Constitution and the Texas Constitution protect the defendant against self-incrimination. CCrP §38.08 states that:

> Any defendant in a criminal action shall be permitted to testify in his own behalf therein, but the failure of any defendant to so testify shall not be taken as a circumstance against him, nor shall the same be alluded to or commented on by counsel in the cause.

Rebuttal and Surrebuttal

After the defense has presented its evidence, the prosecution is entitled to present a **rebuttal** case. At this time, the prosecutor may present evidence in response to the case presented by the defense. The defense may also be entitled to present a **surrebuttal** case, which involves presenting evidence after the prosecution has completed the rebuttal. However, this is at the discretion of the trial court.

Closing Arguments

Once all the evidence is presented, each side is given the opportunity to make a **closing argument** or **summation**, which is addressed directly to the jury. In the closing arguments, each attorney reviews and summarizes the evidence that best supports his or her side of case, discusses any inferences that may be drawn from that evidence, and points out weaknesses in the opponent's case. In Texas, the defense presents closing arguments first, with the goal of trying to persuade the jury to acquit the defendant. When the defense has completed its closing arguments, the prosecution has the right to make the concluding address to the jury, to try to persuade the jury to convict the defendant. Closing arguments are optional for both the prosecution and defense.

Charging the Jury

After the closing arguments are completed, the judge has the opportunity to provide instructions to the jury regarding any legal issues or points of law which are applicable to the case. This step is known as **charging the jury** or **jury instruction**. The judge may not sum up the evidence or make comments on the credibility of witnesses or the guilt of the defendant. S/he may only instruct the jury as to what law or laws must be applied to the evidence of the specific case.

Jury Deliberation and Verdict Rendition

After the judge has given instructions to the jury, the jury retires to the jury room for **deliberation**. At this time, the jurors discuss the case and attempt to come to agreement on a verdict concerning the guilt or innocence of the defendant. Texas requires that all the jurors unanimously agree on a guilty verdict before the defendant can be convicted of a crime. If the jurors are unable to agree on a verdict after a reasonable period of time, they are considered to be a "**hung jury**." If this happens, the judge will declare a **mistrial** and the case may have to be retried in front of a new jury.

If the jurors come to an agreement on a **verdict**, they are returned to the courtroom by the bailiff and the verdict is read in open court. After the verdict is rendered, the jurors must be collectively asked whether this is their verdict. In addition, either the defense or the prosecution is entitled to request a poll of the individual members of the jury to ensure that each member of the jury agrees with the verdict and that no member was coerced or intimidated into agreeing, or agreed simply out of exhaustion. If in either the collective or individual poll, any juror responds negatively, the court must refuse to accept the verdict and direct the jury to resume deliberations.

If the verdict of the jury is not guilty, the trial is over and the defendant must be immediately discharged from custody and is entitled to the return of any bail money and the exoneration of any sureties. The trial court judge is required to accept a verdict of not guilty. Because of the state and federal constitutional protections against double jeopardy, the defendant may never be tried in state court for those same charges.

Proceedings Between the Verdict and the Sentence

After a verdict of guilty is rendered, and before the sentencing phase of the trial, the defendant may make a **post-trial motion** to set aside or modify the verdict. If the judge sets aside the verdict, the defendant may be entitled to a dismissal, a reduction of the charges, or a new trial. These motions are rarely granted.

The Sentence

If the defendant is found guilty, s/he will be sentenced by a judge. In most cases, the judge who presided over the trial will also pronounce the sentence, although in some situations it may be necessary for sentence to be pronounced by a different judge. The sentencing process is discussed in more detail in Chapter 6.

Appeals

After the conclusion of the trial, the defendant may have the option of **appealing** the conviction. In most cases, an appeal does not involve retrying a case or even re-examining the factual issues surrounding the crime. It only involves an examination or review of the legal issues involved in the case. The purpose of an appeal is to make certain that the defendant received a fair trial, that s/he was not deprived of any constitutional rights at any time, and that no errors were committed at the trial that require an **acquittal** or a **retrial**. In most cases, if a defendant wins on appeal, s/he will be retried. In some cases (although this is fairly rare), the case may be reversed and the defendant acquitted. In general, the defendant has the right to appeal regardless of the crime of which s/he was convicted, the sentence that was imposed upon the defendant, and whether the defendant was convicted by a jury or after a plea of guilty.

In some cases, the defendant may be asked to give up his or her right to appeal as a part of the plea bargain. However, even if this is the case, the defendant may be permitted to have the appellate court review certain issues regarding the case.

NOTES

1. Court Structure of Texas (http://www.courts.state.tx.us/publicinfo/crt_stru.htm)
2. See 28 U.S.C. 124
3. United States Court of Appeals, 5th Circuit home page (http://www.ca5.uscourts.gov/)
4. Texas Constitution, Article 5, Section 2
5. Texas Constitution, Article 5, Section 4
6. *Texas Judicial System Annual Report - Fiscal Year 2002.* Available online at: http://www.courts.state.tx.us/publicinfo/annual_reports.asp
7. Texas Judiciary Online: Texas Courts of Appeals (http://www.courts.state.tx.us/appcourt.asp)
8. *Texas Judicial System Annual Report, op cit.*
9. Texas Constitution, Article 5, Section 7
10. *Texas Judicial System Annual Report, op cit.*
11. Texas Constitution, Article 5, Section 15
12. *Ibid*
13. Texas Judiciary Online: Constitutional County Courts (http://www.courts.state.tx.us/trial/constit.asp)
14. Texas Judiciary Online: County Courts at Law (http://www.courts.state.tx.us/trial/catlaw.asp)
15. Texas Judiciary Online: Statutory Probate Courts (http://www.courts.state.tx.us/trial/probate.asp)
16. *Texas Judicial System Annual Report, op cit.*
17. Texas Judiciary Online: Texas Municipal Courts (http://www.courts.state.tx.us/trial/municour.asp)
18. Texas Constitution, Article 5, Section 18
19. *Texas Judicial System Annual Report, op cit.*
20. Texas Judiciary Online: Texas Justice of the Peace Courts (http://www.courts.state.tx.us/trial/jpcourts.asp)
21. Texas Judiciary Online: The Texas Office of Court Administration (http://www.courts.state.tx.us/oca/index.asp)
22. *Ibid*

23. State Commission on Judicial Conduct web site (http://www.scjc.state.tx.us/index.php)
24. Texas Constitution, Article 5, Section 1-a
25. State Commission on Judicial Conduct, *2002 Annual Report*
26. The State Bar of Texas web site (http://www.texasbar.com/)
27. CcrP 15.01
28. *Stack v. Boyle*, 342 U.S. 1 (1951)
29. Texas Constitution, Article 1, Section 11
30. CCrP 21.20
31. CCrP 21.01
32. CcrP 27.02(5)
33. CCrP 29.01 et seq.
34. CCrP 31.01 et seq.
35. CCrP 28.01(6)
36. Texas Constitution, Article I, Section 10
37. CCrP 32A.02 Sec.4
38. CCrP 32A.02 Sec.3
39. See both the 6th Amendment to the U.S. Constitution and Article 1 Section 10 of the Texas Constitution
40. CCrP 33.01
41. CCrP 35.16(a)
42. CCrP 35.16(b)
43. CCrP 35.14
44. CCrP 35.15
45. CCrP 35.261
46. CCrP 35.22

CHAPTER 6

SENTENCING IN TEXAS

INTRODUCTION

After a criminal defendant pleads guilty or is found guilty in court by a judge or jury, the judge must impose a sentence of punishment upon the offender. A **sentence** is defined as

> that part of the judgment, or order revoking a suspension of the imposition of a sentence, that orders that the punishment be carried into execution in the manner prescribed by law.[1]

In every case in which a conviction has been entered, the court is required to pronounce sentence. If the defendant has been found guilty on multiple counts, the court must pronounce sentence on each count. In a felony case, the sentence must be pronounced in open court, in the presence of the defendant, although in a misdemeanor case, the judgment and sentence may be pronounced in the defendant's absence. In all cases, the judge determines the final sentence.

TYPES OF SENTENCES

A variety of sentences may be imposed upon convicted offenders in Texas. Sentences acceptable in the Texas courts include:

- fines
- restitution
- community service
- community supervision (formerly called probation)
- other community-based or intermediate sanctions (e.g., boot camp, house arrest with electronic monitoring, shock incarceration)
- incarceration in a jail or prison
- death

Combinations of these sentences are also allowed. For example, a judge may order both imprisonment and a fine, or order the offender to pay a fine as well as victim restitution. However, the judge has only a limited amount of discretion when imposing a sentence. The judge must follow the authorized punishments outlined in Chapter 12 of the Texas Penal Code.

THE PRESENTENCE REPORT

After a defendant is found guilty of a crime, either by pleading guilty at arraignment or by conviction at trial, he or she will be sentenced by the court. In most cases, the judge will order the preparation of a **presentence report**. This report contains information about the offender's background and about the circumstances of the crime.

According to CCrP §42.12, Sec.9(b), the judge is not required to order a presentence report in a misdemeanor case if:

(1) the defendant requests that a report not be made and the judge agrees to the request; or
(2) the judge finds that there is sufficient information in the record to permit the meaningful exercise of sentencing discretion and the judge explains this finding on the record.

In most cases, if the defendant is being sentenced for a felony, a presentence report must be prepared prior to sentencing. However, if one of the following conditions holds, the report does not have to be prepared unless requested by the defendant:

(1) punishment is to be assessed by a jury;
(2) the defendant is convicted of or enters a plea of guilty or nolo contendere to capital murder;
(3) the only available punishment is imprisonment; or
(4) the judge is informed that a plea bargain agreement exists, under which the defendant agrees to a punishment of imprisonment, and the judge intends to follow the agreement.[2]

The main contents of the presentence report are outlined in CCrP 42.12, Sec.9(a), and include:

- the circumstances of the offense with which the defendant has been charged

- the amount of restitution that is considered necessary to adequately compensate the victim

- the defendant's criminal and social history

- any other information requested by the judge that relates to the defendant or the offense

- a proposed client supervision plan that describes programs and sanctions to be provided by the corrections department if the judge suspended the sentence or deferred adjudication

Prior to sentencing, both the defendant and the defense counsel have the right to read the presentence report, to comment upon it, and to present evidence claiming factual inaccuracies in the report or the presentence investigation.[3]

DETERMINATE AND INDETERMINATE SENTENCING

A **determinate sentence** is a flat or fixed-term prison sentence for an offense. Conversely, a sentence that includes a range of time between a specified minimum and maximum is known as an **indeterminate sentence**. In other words, a sentence requiring an offender to spend three to five years in a state prison is an indeterminate sentence. A sentence that states a specific fixed period of time to be served, such as years in prison, is a determinate sentence.

In Texas, the punishments assigned to each type of felony or misdemeanor are specified by statute and, where imprisonment is an option, include maximum and minimum sentences that may be imposed. When the court sentences an offender to a term of imprisonment, the judge must impose a determinate sentence within this range. For example, the statutory sentence of imprisonment for a second degree felony is a term of not less than two years nor more than 20 years.[4] The court, when sentencing an offender convicted of a second degree felony to a term of imprisonment, must impose a sentence consisting of a specific fixed period of time within that range. The judge may not sentence the offender to a term of, for example, four to six years, even though that range falls within the range specified in the statute.

CONCURRENT VERSUS CUMULATIVE SENTENCES

If an offender is convicted of multiple offenses, the court must impose a separate sentence for each offense. If the sentences imposed involve terms of imprisonment in a county jail or a state prison, the court has the option of requiring the sentences to be served either concurrently or cumulatively. **Concurrent sentences** are served at the same time. **Cumulative sentences** (sometimes known as **consecutive sentences**) are served in succession, one after the other. For example, if an offender is convicted of two counts of a second degree felony, and receives sentences of four years in a state prison for each count, to be served concurrently, both sentences are satisfied after a total of four years. If, however, the sentences are to be served consecutively, the offender must serve a total of eight years to satisfy both sentences.

In most situations, the court has considerable discretion in deciding whether multiple sentences will be served concurrently or consecutively. However, in some circumstances, the law sets forth specific requirements and removes the discretion from the court. For example, CCRP 42.08(b) states that:

> If a defendant is sentenced for an offense committed while the defendant was an inmate in the institutional division of the Texas Department of Criminal Justice and the defendant has not completed the sentence he was serving at the time of the offense, the judge shall order the sentence for the subsequent offense to commence immediately on completion of the sentence for the original offense.

Thus, in this situation, the sentences for the new crime and the old crime must be served consecutively, rather than concurrently.

SENTENCES OF IMPRISONMENT

According to the Texas Penal Code, crimes are classified into categories which are based on the relative seriousness of the offense. Each category of crimes has an associated punishment. Felonies in Texas are classified into five categories, which are listed in Pen §12.04. The associated punishments for these crimes are defined in Pen §12.31 through Pen §12.35. All felony offenses are punishable by a term of imprisonment in a state penitentiary or, in the case of a state jail felony, in a state jail facility.

Misdemeanor offenses are also classified into categories by level of seriousness. According to Pen §12.03(b), if an offense is listed as a misdemeanor in the statutes, but the specific class or degree of the crime is not specified, the crime is considered to be a Class C misdemeanor. The associated punishments for these crimes are defined in Pen §12.21 through Pen §12.35. Class A and Class B misdemeanors may be punishable by a term of imprisonment in a county jail but Class C misdemeanors do not include incarceration as a possible sanction.

Chapter 2 discusses the classification of crimes into felonies and misdemeanors, and the authorized sanctions for each category, in more detail.

SENTENCING HABITUAL AND/OR REPEAT OFFENDERS

According to the Texas Penal Code, an offender with prior convictions may be given a more severe sentence. The sentencing of repeat and habitual felony offenders is discussed in Pen §12.42. For example, an offender who is convicted of a second degree felony and who has a prior felony conviction will be punished for a first degree felony.[5] In the case of an offender convicted of a state jail felony, if s/he has previously been convicted of two state jail felonies, the offender will be punished as if convicted of a third degree felony.[6]

In most cases, if the defendant is a first-time repeat offender, the punishment is increased one punishment level (e.g., from a second degree felony to a first degree felony). If the repeat offender is convicted of a first degree felony, the minimum term of imprisonment is increased to 15 years. Generally, if the defendant is a habitual offender, meaning s/he has at least two prior felony convictions, s/he is subject to a minimum term of imprisonment of 25 years and a maximum sentence of 99 years in prison or life imprisonment.

Pen §12.43 outlines sentence enhancements for repeat and habitual misdemeanor offenders. In most cases, the minimum term of imprisonment is increased if the offender has certain prior convictions. If the offender convicted of a Class A misdemeanor has a prior conviction for a Class A misdemeanor or for any felony, the minimum term is increased to 90 days. If the offender is convicted of a Class B misdemeanor and has a prior conviction of at least that level, the minimum term is increased to 30 days.

OTHER SENTENCING ALTERNATIVES

Restitution, Reparation, and Fines

Several types of sentences that may be imposed require the offender to make some type of financial payment, either to the court or to the victim. A **fine** is a monetary payment made to the state as a punishment for an offense. **Restitution** involves repaying the victim for a loss sustained as a result of the crime. **Reparation** involves compensating the victim for some harm that resulted from the crime. The death of the victim does not end the offender's requirement to pay restitution or reparation. If the victim dies before the payments are completed, all remaining payments must be made to the deceased's estate.

For some crimes, such as Class C misdemeanors, a fine may be the only penalty imposed on the offender by the court. However, as discussed above, for most felonies and misdemeanors, the court has the option of sentencing an offender to both a fine and a term of imprisonment.

Texas, like most states, is attempting to increase the use of restitution and reparation. CCrP §42.037 discusses the issue of restitution, stating that:

> (a) In addition to any fine authorized by law, the court that sentences a defendant convicted of an offense may order the defendant to make restitution to any victim of the offense. If the court does not order restitution or orders partial restitution under this subsection, the court shall state on the record the reasons for not making the order or for the limited order.

Restitution may include returning damaged, lost, or destroyed property to a victim, paying the victim the value of the property, paying medical costs (including therapy and rehabilitation), reimbursing the victim for lost income, or paying funeral and other expenses. The actual amount of the restitution is determined by the court, which also sets a time period in which restitution must be paid. According to CCrP §42.037(g)(2), if payment is to be made in installments or within a specific period of time:

> The end of the period or the last installment may not be later than:

> (A) the end of the period of probation, if probation is ordered;
> (B) five years after the end of the term of imprisonment imposed, if the court does not order probation; or
> (C) five years after the date of sentencing in any other case.

If the court does not specify a time period, restitution must be made immediately.

Community Service

According to CCrP §42.036(a):

> A court may require a defendant,..., to serve all or part of a sentence of confinement or period of confinement required as a condition of community supervision in county jail by performing community service rather than by being confined in county jail unless the sentence of confinement was imposed by the jury in the case.

This statute does not apply to defendants convicted of certain crimes involving intoxication, such as driving while intoxicated.

A sentence of **community service** must specify the number of hours that must be served as well as the specific agency or organization for which the defendant will work. Offenders may only be sentenced to perform community service for government agencies or nonprofit organizations that meet certain specified statutory criteria.[7] Each eight hours of community service performed is considered to be the equivalent of one day served in jail.[8] In most cases, a defendant who is employed may not be ordered to perform more than 16 hours of community service per week, while an unemployed defendant may be ordered to perform up to 32 hours per week and required to spend the rest of the weeks attempting to obtain employment.[9]

Community Supervision

Community supervision or **probation** is discussed in CCrP §42.12. The statute defines community supervision as:

> the placement of a defendant by a court under a continuum of programs and sanctions, with conditions imposed by the court for a specified period during which:
> (A) criminal proceedings are deferred without an adjudication of guilt; or
> (B) a sentence of imprisonment or confinement, imprisonment and fine, or confinement and fine, is probated and the imposition of sentence is suspended in whole or in part.[10]

The topic of probation will be discussed in more detail in Chapter 8 of this supplement.

VICTIM'S RIGHTS AND SERVICES

General Rights of Crime Victims

In 1989, the Texas Constitution was amended to include a **Bill of Rights for Crime Victims**. The Constitution states that:

(a) A crime victim has the following rights:
  (1) the right to be treated with fairness and with respect for the victim's dignity and privacy throughout the criminal justice process; and
  (2) the right to be reasonably protected from the accused throughout the criminal justice process.

(b) On the request of a crime victim, the crime victim has the following rights:
  (1) the right to notification of court proceedings;
  (2) the right to be present at all public court proceedings related to the offense, unless the victim is to testify and the court determines that the victim's testimony would be materially affected if the victim hears other testimony at the trial;
  (3) the right to confer with a representative of the prosecutor's office;
  (4) the right to restitution; and
  (5) the right to information about the conviction, sentence, imprisonment, and release of the accused.

(c) The legislature may enact laws to define the term "victim" and to enforce these and other rights of crime victims.

(d) The state, through its prosecuting attorney, has the right to enforce the rights of crime victims.

(e) The legislature may enact laws to provide that a judge, attorney for the state, peace officer, or law enforcement agency is not liable for a failure or inability to provide a right enumerated in this section. The failure or inability of any person to provide a right or service enumerated in this section may not be used by a defendant in a criminal case as a ground for appeal or post-conviction writ of habeas corpus. A victim or guardian or legal representative of a victim has standing to enforce the rights enumerated in this section but does not have standing to participate as a party in a criminal proceeding or to contest the disposition of any charge.

The rights of crime victims are discussed in more detail in Chapter 56 of the Code of Criminal Procedure. According to CCrP 56.02(a), crime victims, including the guardian of a victim or the close relative of a deceased victim, are entitled to certain specified rights within the criminal justice system. These include:

(1) the right to receive from law enforcement agencies adequate protection from harm and threats of harm arising from cooperation with prosecution efforts;

(2) the right to have the magistrate take the safety of the victim or his family into consideration as an element in fixing the amount of bail for the accused;

(3) the right, if requested, to be informed

 (A) by the attorney representing the state of relevant court proceedings, including appellate proceedings, and to be informed if those proceedings have been cancelled or rescheduled prior to the event; and

 (B) by an appellate court of decisions of the court, after the decisions are entered but before the decisions are made public;

(4) the right to be informed, when requested, by a peace officer concerning the defendant's right to bail and the procedures in criminal investigations and by the district attorney's office concerning the general procedures in the criminal justice system, including general procedures in guilty plea negotiations and arrangements, restitution, and the appeals and parole process;

(5) the right to provide pertinent information to a probation department conducting a presentencing investigation concerning the impact of the offense on the victim and his family by testimony, written statement, or any other manner prior to any sentencing of the offender;

(6) the right to receive information regarding compensation to victims of crime...

(7) the right to be informed, upon request, of parole procedures, to participate in the parole process, to be notified, if requested, of parole proceedings concerning a defendant in the victim's case, to provide to the Board of Pardons and Paroles for inclusion in the defendant's file information to be considered by the board prior to the parole of any defendant convicted of any crime subject to this Act, and to be notified, if requested, of the defendant's release;

(8) the right to be provided with a waiting area, separate or secure from other witnesses, including the offender and relatives of the offender, before testifying in any proceeding concerning the offender; if a separate waiting area is not available, other safeguards should be taken to minimize the victim's contact with the offender and the offender's relatives and witnesses, before and during court proceedings;

(9) the right to prompt return of any property of the victim that is held by a law enforcement agency or the attorney for the state as evidence when the property is no longer required for that purpose;

(10) the right to have the attorney for the state notify the employer of the victim, if requested, of the necessity of the victim's cooperation and testimony in a proceeding that may necessitate the absence of the victim from work for good cause; and

(11) the right to counseling, on request, regarding acquired immune deficiency syndrome (AIDS) and human immunodeficiency virus (HIV) infection and testing for acquired immune deficiency syndrome (AIDS), human immunodeficiency virus (HIV) infection, antibodies to HIV, or infection with any other probable causative agent of AIDS, if the offense is an offense under Section 21.11(a)(1), 22.011, or 22.021, Penal Code.

(12) the right to request victim-offender mediation coordinated by the victim services division of the Texas Department of Criminal Justice; and

(13) the right to be informed of the uses of a victim impact statement and the statement's purpose in the criminal justice system, to complete the victim impact statement, and to have the victim impact statement considered:

    (A) by the attorney representing the state and the judge before sentencing or before a plea bargain agreement is accepted; and

    (B) by the Board of Pardons and Paroles before an inmate is released on parole.

In addition, crime victims have the right to be present at all public court proceedings that are related to the crime.

Victim Impact Statements

A **Victim Impact Statement** is a written report or verbal statement that is given to the sentencing judge and that describes the effects of the crime upon the victim. In Texas, the victim impact statement includes the following information:

- the name of the victim or victim's legal guardian, or the name of a guardian or close relative of a deceased victim
- the address and telephone number of the victim, guardian, or relative
- information on the economic loss suffered by the victim, guardian, or relative as a result of the crime
- information as to any physical or psychological injury suffered by the victim, guardian, or relative as a result of the crime
- information on any psychological services requested as a result of the crime
- information on any change in the victim's, guardian's, or relative's personal welfare or family relationships as a result of the crime

- information as to the victim's, guardian's, or relative's wishes regarding future notification of parole hearings for the defendant

- any other information, other than facts related to the commission of the crime, that relates to the impact of the offense on the victim, guardian, or relative[11]

The court is not allowed to see the victim impact statement until after the defendant has been found guilty or adjudication has been deferred.[12]

The Right to Restitution

When pronouncing sentence, the judge is required to consider imposing **victim restitution** as an element of the sentence. This generally involves requiring the offender to pay a sum of money to the victim as a consequence of the crime. For example, the offender may be required to reimburse the victim for medical expenses or lost wages . Restitution may also be in a nonmonetary form. The right to restitution is guaranteed in the Texas Constitution's Bill of Rights of Crime Victims.[13]

The defendant may be ordered to pay restitution in a lump sum or to make payments over a period of time. Restitution may be ordered even if the judge sentences the offender to a fine or a term of imprisonment in jail or prison.

Even if the judge has ordered the offender to make restitution, the victim still has the right to file a civil suit against the offender for damages that are in excess of the amount paid in restitution.

The Right to Compensation

In addition to restitution, victims may be eligible for **compensation**. The **Texas Crime Victims' Compensation Program**, which is administered by the Office of the Attorney General, provides benefits to victims and their families who have no other way to pay for expenses that result from a crime. The Crime Victims' Compensation Fund is considered to be a last resort for victims, to be used only if there are no other alternative sources to pay for certain specified victim expenses. Therefore, if the victim has medical insurance which will cover the cost of medical care, or long-term disability insurance to cover loss of wages, the victim may not request victim compensation for these costs. If the offender is sentenced to pay restitution to the victim, the victim may not also receive compensation from the Fund for the same expenses. In addition, if a victim receives compensation from the Fund, and the offender is later ordered by the court to make restitution, the victim may be required to reimburse the fund. Similarly, if the victim receives money from a civil suit to cover crime-related expenses, s/he may have to reimburse the Fund for any prior compensation money already paid out by the Fund.

To qualify for victim compensation, certain basic requirements must be met. These include:

- the crime must occur in Texas to a resident of Texas or the U.S., or must involve a Texas resident who has been victimized in a state or country that does not have compensation benefits for which the victim is eligible

- the crime must be reported to the appropriate law enforcement agency within a reasonable period of time

- the application for compensation must be filed within three years of the date of the crime, although this time may be extended if there is good cause (e.g., the victim's age, physical incapacity, or mental incapacity)

- the victim must cooperate with the police or other appropriate law enforcement agencies.[14]

Crimes covered by the Crime Victims' Compensation Fund include those involving "criminally injurious conduct," which is defined as:

> conduct that:
> (A) occurs or is attempted;
> (B) poses a substantial threat of personal injury or death;
> (C) is punishable by fine, imprisonment, or death, or would be punishable by fine, imprisonment, or death if the person engaging in the conduct possessed capacity to commit the conduct; and
> (D) does not arise out of the ownership, maintenance, or use of a motor vehicle, aircraft, or water vehicle, unless the conduct is intended to cause personal injury or death or the conduct is in violation of Section 550.021, Transportation Code, or one or more of the following sections of the Penal Code:
> (I) ..manslaughter;
> (ii) ...criminally negligent homicide;
> (iii) ...aggravated assault;
> (iv) ...driving while intoxicated;
> (v) ...flying while intoxicated;
> (vi) ...boating while intoxicated;
> (vii) ...intoxication assault; or
> (viii) ...intoxication manslaughter.[15]

If the victim's behavior contributed to the crime, compensation may be reduced or denied. Compensation benefits will be denied if the victim participated in the crime knowingly or willingly, if the victim is the offender or an accomplice, if the victim was incarcerated or on probation or parole for a felony that involved criminally injurious conduct at the time of the crime, or if the victim knowingly or intentionally provided the attorney general with false or forged information.[16]

Texas provides victim compensation benefits up to a total of $50,000. Expenses which are eligible for compensation (if they are related to the crime) include medical costs, psychiatric care or counseling, loss of earnings or support, care of a child or dependent, funeral or burial expenses, crime scene clean-up, replacement costs for certain types of property, and other expenses specified by the Compensation Program. Reimbursement for property damage or loss from theft is not an eligible expense under the program.

In FY 2003, over $71 million was paid out to victims of crime. The average amount that was awarded to each victim applicant was $4,491.[17]

NOTES

1. CCrP 42.02
2. CCrP 42.12, Sec.9(g)
3. CCrP 42.12, Sec. 9(d) and 9(e)
4. Pen §12.33(a)
5. Pen §12.42(b)
6. Pen §12.42(a)(1)
7. CCrP 42.036(c)
8. CCrP 42.036(f)
9. CCrP 42.036(e)
10. CCrP 42.12 Sec 2(2)
11. CCrP 56.03(b)
12. CCrP 56.03(f)
13. Texas Constitution, Article I, Section 30(b)(4)
14. Office of the Attorney General - Crime Victim Services (http://www.oag.state.tx.us/victims/victims.shtml)
15. CCrP 56.32(4)
16. Office of the Attorney General - Crime Victim Services, *op cit.*
17. Office of the Attorney General (2003). *Crime Victims' Compensation Program: 2003 Annual Report*. Available online at: http://www.oag.state.tx.us/AG_Publications/pdfs/2003cvc_annual.pdf

CHAPTER 7

CAPITAL PUNISHMENT IN TEXAS

THE HISTORY OF CAPITAL PUNISHMENT IN TEXAS

Between 1819 and 1923, the method of execution used in Texas was hanging, and each county carried out its own executions. However, in 1923, the Texas State Legislature authorized the use of electrocution as the official method of capital punishment in the state. The Legislature also transferred the responsibility for executions to the state, with all executions to be performed at the Huntsville Unit facility. The first state-authorized electrocution was carried out on February 8, 1924 when five inmates were executed. Death Row was moved to Huntsville in 1928 and both Death Row and the state's electric chair remained there until 1965, when all Death Row inmates were moved to the Ellis Unit. In 1999, Death Row inmates were moved to the Terrell Unit.[1]

Between 1924 and 1973, 506 offenders were placed on Death Row in Texas, including three female offenders. A total of 361 of these inmates were electrocuted. All were male. Approximately 63 percent were black, 30 percent were white, and 6 percent were Hispanic.[2]

On June 29, 1972, the U.S. Supreme Court case of *Furman v. Georgia*[3] challenged the constitutionality of capital punishment in the United States. The Court ruled that the death penalty, as it was administered, constituted "cruel and unusual punishment" and therefore was a violation of the Eighth Amendment of the U.S. Constitution. The case struck down death penalty laws throughout the country. At the time of the *Furman v. Georgia* decision, there were a total of 52 men in Texas under a sentence of death. The Governor commuted all death sentences to sentences of life imprisonment and the Texas Death Row was emptied by March, 1973.[4]

In 1973, the Texas State Legislature revised the Penal Code, reinstating the death penalty in Texas as of January 1, 1974. The first offender sentenced under the new statute was placed on Death Row in February, 1974. He committed suicide later that year.[5]

In August 1977, Texas became the first state in the U.S. to change from electrocution to lethal injection as the method of execution. The first inmate in the country to be executed by lethal injection, Charlie Brooks, was put to death in Texas on December 7, 1982. Three years later, in 1985, Texas became the first state in the country to execute a juvenile offender. Charles Rumbaugh was 17 when he committed a robbery and murder He was executed at the age of 28.

Although close friends and relatives of the offender have historically been allowed to attend the execution, it was not until 1995 that the state gave the same right to close relatives and friends of the deceased victim. Currently, five family members or friends of the offender, as well as five family members or friends of the victim, have the right to witness the execution.

In 1998, Karla Faye Tucker became the first woman to be executed by lethal injection. She was also the first woman to be executed in Texas since 1863 and the second woman to be executed in the U.S. since the reinstatement of the death penalty in 1977.

Since the death penalty was reinstated in the United States in 1976[6], Texas has executed more offenders than any other state. Texas also has the largest death row population in the U.S., followed by California and Florida.[7]

CAPITAL OFFENSES

The only death penalty offense that has ever existed in Texas is **capital murder**. Capital murder is basically first degree murder that includes at least one of eight aggravating factors. According to Pen §19.03(a), these aggravating factors include:

(1) the person murders a peace officer or fireman who is acting in the lawful discharge of an official duty and who the person knows is a peace officer or fireman;
(2) the person intentionally commits the murder in the course of committing or attempting to commit kidnapping, burglary, robbery, aggravated sexual assault, arson, obstruction or retaliation, or terroristic threat...;
(3) the person commits the murder for remuneration or the promise of remuneration or employs another to commit the murder for remuneration or the promise of remuneration;
(4) the person commits the murder while escaping or attempting to escape from a penal institution;
(5) the person, while incarcerated in a penal institution, murders another:
   (A) who is employed in the operation of the penal institution; or
   (B) with the intent to establish, maintain, or participate in a combination or in the profits of a combination;
(6) the person:
   (A) while incarcerated for an offense under this section or Section 19.02, murders another; or
   (B) while serving a sentence of life imprisonment or a term of 99 years for an offense under Section 20.04, 22.021, or 29.03, murders another;
(7) the person murders more than one person:
   (A) during the same criminal transaction; or
   (B) during different criminal transactions but the murders are committed pursuant to the same scheme or course of conduct; or
(8) the person murders an individual under six years of age.

The minimum age to receive the death penalty in Texas is 17. Texas does not forbid the execution of mentally retarded offenders.

THE DEATH PENALTY TRIAL AND APPEALS PROCESS

In all cases involving capital murder, the accused must be indicted by a Grand Jury, rather than a prosecutorial information. The accused then goes to an arraignment where s/he enters a formal plea. The court determines whether or not the defendant is indigent and, if necessary, appoints legal counsel to represent the defendant. This counsel must be an attorney qualified to handle a case involving the death penalty. After any pre-trial motions are made and considered, a trial is held to determine the defendant's guilt or innocence of the charge of capital murder. This must be a jury trial rather than a bench trial; a defendant who is charged with a capital felony in which the state plans to seek the death penalty may not waive his or her right to a trial by jury. If the state is seeking the death penalty, the state and the defense are allowed fifteen peremptory challenges each during the jury selection phase. If the death penalty is not being sought, each side is entitled to only ten such challenges.

In all capital cases, the prosecution is required to state prior to trial whether or not it plans to seek the death penalty as punishment for the crime.[8] This information must also be provided to prospective jury members. The prosecution has the right to make a challenge for cause if:

> the juror has conscientious scruples in regard to the infliction of the punishment of death for crime, in a capital case, where the State is seeking the death penalty.[9]

Therefore, the prosecution is permitted to ask each prospective juror his or her views on capital punishment during the *voir dire*. If the state does not plan to seek the death penalty, all prospective jurors must be informed of this fact and told that, upon conviction, a sentence of life imprisonment is mandatory.[10]

If the defendant is found guilty of capital murder, the only possible sentences are death or life imprisonment.[11] If the state is seeking the death penalty, a separate sentencing hearing will be held to determine whether the defendant will be sentenced to life imprisonment or death. When possible, the sentence will be determined by the same jury that convicted the defendant.

In Texas, the conviction of a capital crime, and a sentence of death, are automatically appealed to the Court of Criminal Appeals. Because this appeal is mandatory, the Court does not have the discretion to refuse the appeal. The full complement of nine justices must convene for all death penalty cases. If the Court finds against the offender, a writ of certiorari may be filed to the United States Supreme Court to appeal the conviction or the sentence. This appeal must be based on United States constitutional grounds.

In Texas, the governor has the power of **executive clemency**, which is the right to grant a full or a conditional pardon, a full pardon based on innocence, a commutation of sentence, a remission of a fine or forfeiture that resulted from a criminal conviction, an emergency medical reprieve, or a thirty-day reprieve of execution. A reprieve is not a pardon or commutation of a sentence. It merely delays or temporarily suspends the execution. With the exception of the 30-reprieve, the governor can only grant executive clemency upon a recommendation from the **Texas Board of Pardons and Paroles**.[12]

All requests for executive clemency must be filed with the Texas Board of Pardons and Paroles, which reviews the case and renders a decision on the request. If the Board recommends executive clemency, the case is passed to the state governor, who has the right to accept or reject the Board's recommendation. If the Board denies the request for clemency, a Death Row inmate has the right to request a one-time, thirty-day reprieve of execution from the state governor, who has the constitutional authority to issue such a reprieve without a recommendation from the Board. The purpose of such a reprieve is, in most cases, to give the Board additional time to conduct a full hearing on the case.[13]

CAPITAL PUNISHMENT IN TEXAS TODAY

Death Row in Texas

Offenders sentenced to death are confined in segregated units maintained by the Institutional Division of the Texas Department of Criminal Justice. Male death row offenders are confined at the Polunsky Unit, near Livingston, Texas. Female offenders are held in a separate death row facility in Mountain View, near Gatesville, Texas.[14]

The standard death row cell is a single-person cell that is 60 square feet and has a window. It is not air conditioned. Inmates on death row do not participate in communal recreation, but are recreated individually. They may spend up to 23 hours per day in their cells. They are not allowed access to television but some offenders, depending on their level of custody, may be allowed a radio. There are three levels of custody, depending on the inmate's record of behavior. Inmates receive a regular diet but do not eat with the general prison population. It costs approximately $61.58 per day to incarcerate an inmate on death row.[15]

Visitation for Death Row inmates is limited. Individuals allowed access to Death Row inmates include:

- the inmate's physician
- the inmate's lawyer
- the inmate's clergyperson
- relatives and friends of the condemned inmate[16]

Executions in Texas

In Texas, all executions are held after 6:00 p.m on the day set for the execution.[17] Only certain individuals are allowed to attend as witnesses to the execution. These include the following:

- the executioner and any others needed to assist in the execution
- the Board of Directors of the Texas Department of Corrections
- two physicians (including the prison physician)
- the condemned offender's spiritual advisor
- chaplains of the Texas Department of Corrections
- the sheriff or county judge of the county in which the Department of Corrections is located (Walker County)
- up to five family members or friends of the offender[18]

The statute also states that no convict is allowed to witness executions. In addition, since 1996, relatives and friends of the deceased victim have also been permitted to witness the execution.[19]

The lethal injection used to execute inmates in Texas includes three separate drugs:

- a lethal dose of sodium thiopental which sedates the individual

- a dose of pancuronium bromide, a muscle relaxant which collapses the diaphragm and lungs

- a dose of potassium chloride which stops the heart from beating

The total cost of the drugs used is $86.08. The entire lethal injection process lasts approximately seven minutes from the start of the procedure until the offender is pronounced dead.[20]

Death Row Statistics

As of March, 2004, there were a total of 452 offenders on death row in Texas. This includes 9 women and 443 men. Of these, approximately 40 percent are black, 32 percent white, and 27 percent Hispanic. The average length of stay on Death Row prior to execution is 10.43 years. The longest stay on Death Row was approximately 24 years and the shortest stay was 252 days. The average age of executed offenders is 39 years. The youngest inmates to be executed were Jay Pinkerton and Jesse De La Rosa, who were both 24 years of age at the time of their executions. The oldest inmate to be executed was William Chappell, who was 66 when he was executed on November 20, 2002. The last woman to be executed was Betty Betts, who was put to death on February 24, 2000 for the murder of her fifth husband.[21]

Since the death penalty was officially reinstated in the United States in 1976, Texas has executed more offenders than any other state in the country. Between 1976, when executions resumed throughout the United States, and July 1, 2003, a total of 859 inmates were put to death in the U.S. Of these 305 (35.5 percent) were executed in Texas.[22] In the year 2002, there were 65 executions in the U.S, of which 24 (37 percent) took place in Texas.[23]

NOTES

1. Texas Department of Criminal Justice - Death Row Information (http://www.tdcj.state.tx.us/stat/deathrow.htm)
2. *Ibid*
3. *Furman v. Georgia*, 408 U.S. 238 (1972)
4. Texas Department of Criminal Justice - Death Row Information, *op cit.*
5. *Ibid*
6. *Gregg v. Georgia*, 428 U.S. 153 (1976)
7. Texas Department of Criminal Justice - Death Row Information, *op cit.*
8. Pen §12.31(b)
9. CCrP 35.16(b)(1)
10. Pen §12.31(b)
11. Pen §12.31(a)
12. Texas Board of Pardons and Paroles - Executive Clemency in Texas (http://www.tdcj.state.tx.us/bpp/exec_clem/exec_clem.html)
13. *Ibid*
14. Texas Department of Criminal Justice - Death Row Information, *op cit.*
15. *Ibid*
16. CCrP 43.17
17. CCrP §43.14
18. CCrP §43.20
19. Texas Department of Criminal Justice - Death Row Information, *op cit.*
20. *Ibid*
21. *Ibid*
22. NAACP Legal Defense and Educational Fund, Inc. *Death Row U.S.A.: Summer 2003.* (http://www.deathpenaltyinfo.org/DEATHROWUSArecent.pdf)
23. Death Penalty Information Center (http://www.deathpenaltyinfo.org/dpicreg.html)

CHAPTER 8

CORRECTIONS IN TEXAS

INTRODUCTION

The agency primarily responsible for the administration of the state's correctional program, and for the confinement, supervision, punishment, rehabilitation, and reintegration into society of convicted offenders, is the **Texas Department of Criminal Justice**, which operates state prisons and state jails, administers parole, and oversees community supervision programs (formerly known as adult probation). The Department's operation is governed by the **Texas Board of Criminal Justice**.

THE TEXAS BOARD OF CRIMINAL JUSTICE

The **Texas Board of Criminal Justice** (TBCJ) oversees the operation of the Texas Department of Criminal Justice (TDCJ). The TBCJ has nine members who are appointed by the governor with the advice and consent of the state senate. One member is designated by the governor to be the chairman of the TBCJ. Members of the TBCJ serve staggered six-year terms and are not compensated for their service on the Board, although they may be reimbursed for expenses.[1] Board members go through a training program that must comply with the requirements outlined in Section 492.0031 of the Government Code (GC). These include providing the member with information on:

- the legislation that created the TDCJ and the TBCJ
- programs operated by the TDCJ
- the roles and functions of the TDCJ
- the rules of the TDCJ
- the TDCJ current budget
- the results of the most recent formal audit of the TDCJ
- the requirements of various laws relating to public officials
- all applicable ethics policies

The Board has a variety of responsibilities, including hiring the executive director of the TDCJ and setting department rules and policies. The Board also acts as the Board of Trustees for the Windham School System, which is located within the TDCJ. They hire the school system superintendent and provide general guidance and oversight. The Board, which is headquartered in Austin, meets at least four times a year.

THE TEXAS DEPARTMENT OF CRIMINAL JUSTICE

The **Texas Department of Criminal Justice** (TDCJ) is the state agency responsible for the oversight of all inmates held in state correctional facilities. In most cases, the Department is responsible only for adult offenders, individuals who are at least 17 years of age. The Department operates state prisons, state jails, and state parole, as well as overseeing community supervision. The mission of the Department is defined by statute:

> The mission of the department is to provide public safety, promote positive change in offender behavior, reintegrate offenders into society, and assist victims of crime.[2]

The Department is divided into a large number of separate divisions. Some of the most important are discussed below.

The Correctional Institutions Division

In 2003, the TDCJ created the **Correctional Institutions Division** by merging the Institutional Division, the Operations Division, the Private Facilities Division, and the State Jail Division. The Correctional Institutions Division (CI Division) is the largest division in the Department and is responsible for all adult felony and state jail felony offenders sentenced to confinement in prison, as well as for a variety of support operations, and for the administration of privately-operated facilities.[3]

As of August 31, 2002, the division operated a total of 60 state prison facilities, including 51 prison units, three psychiatric facilities, two pre-release facilities, two medical facilities, one mentally retarded offender program, and one substance abuse facility. These facilities contain five high-security units as well as additional medical facilities, boot camps, and work camps located within some of these facilities. The division is also responsible for housing offenders who are awaiting transfer to prison. These inmates are housed in 13 transfer facilities operated by the division, as well as in state jails and contract transfer facilities. The division also has contracts with a number of privately-operated prison facilities to house offenders.[4]

On August 31, 2001, there were 125,655 offenders incarcerated in prison facilities in Texas. (including those in both state- and privately-run institutions). An additional 449 offenders were incarcerated on death row. Of those offenders in the general population (not on death row), 95 percent were male and 5 percent were female. Approximately 41 percent of the incarcerated offenders were black, 30 percent were white, and 28 percent were Hispanic. The average age was 36 years. Approximately 53 percent of the offenders were incarcerated for a violent offense and 42 percent had a record of prior confinement in a Texas state prison.[5]

Incarcerated offenders are provided with a variety of educational opportunities. Basic adult education is available for those offenders who function at or below a sixth-grade level and GED programs are also provided. Offenders with limited English-speaking abilities may participate in English as a Second Language programs and offenders with disabilities may qualify for special education services. In addition, a variety of vocational classes are available. Classes are offered through the **Windham School District** (WSD), which is the only fully accredited school system within a prison in the United States. Offenders who have a high school diploma, or who have earned a GED may have access to college-level academic or vocational classes through local universities and colleges. Offenders who earn the privilege of taking college courses must reimburse the state for all tuition and fees after they are released from incarceration.[6] During the 2001-2002 school year, WSD operated a total of 88 schools and served over 83,000 students. Almost 77, 000 were enrolled in academic courses and 16,000 in vocational programs.[7]

Offenders incarcerated in state prison facilities receive all essential items from the prison. They are not allowed to possess money while in prison but they may open a trust account into which family and friends may deposit money. These funds may be used by the inmates to make purchases from the unit commissary. In general, offenders may spend up to $75 every two weeks on ordinary merchandise such as snack foods, toiletries, magazines, and books. They may also purchase special items (fans, radios, clothing, etc.) to which the $75 limit does not apply.[8]

While all prison units in Texas have heating units, only the hospital and psychiatric units have air conditioning during the summer months. Other units have forced air systems that keep inside air moving and bring in fresh air. Ironically, offenders housed in single cell administrative segregation units also have air conditioning. This is because the windows in these cells cannot be opened due to a security concern that weapons or other contraband could be smuggled into these restricted areas through the open window. Thus, in a direct contradiction to the divisional philosophy that privileges must be earned, those offenders housed in administrative segregation for poor behavior have the privilege of air conditioning while offenders housed in the general population do not have this privilege.[9]

The CI Division is also responsible for state jails in Texas. Offenders convicted of state jail felonies, primarily low-level non-violent felonies that include various types of property and drug offenses, may be sentenced to a term of incarceration in a state jail facility for up to two years for each offense. State jails also serve as transfer facilities for minimum security offenders awaiting transfer from a local county jail to a state prison unit. There are 17 state jail facilities located throughout the state. Twelve are operated by the state and five are private contract facilities that are supervised by the state jail division. As of August 31, 2002, there were a total of 14,702 offenders housed in state jails. Of these, 78 percent were male and 22 percent female. Approximately 45 percent of these offenders were black, 32 percent were white, and 22 percent were Hispanic. The average age of state jail residents was 31.6 years.[10]

The Community Justice Assistance Division

The **Community Justice Assistance Division** (CJAD) is responsible for administering community supervision in Texas. The term "adult probation" was officially changed to "community supervision" by the Legislature in 1989. CJAD works with community supervision and corrections departments that oversee those offenders who are serving their sentence in the community, rather than serving a sentence of incarceration.[11] Community supervision in Texas is discussed in more detail later in this chapter.

The Parole Division

The **Parole Division** of the TDCJ is responsible for supervising offenders who have been released from prison and who are serving the remainder of their sentence in the community. The division is also responsible for certain pre-release programs, such as the pre-parole transfer program and the work program. The division is not responsible for making release or revocation decisions or for assigning special conditions of parole.[12] Parole in Texas is discussed in more detail later in this chapter.

The Victim Services Division

The **Victim Services Division** provides services to victims and their families to ensure them the opportunity to participate in all phases of the criminal justice system. CCrP §56.02 is known as the Bill of Rights for Texas Crime Victims and outlines the rights of victims, their guardians, and close relatives of deceased victims. Sections of this statute are quoted in Chapter 6.

The division provides a variety of services to victims. The **Victim Notification System** provides written notification to victims of an offender's status after conviction and sentencing. In Fiscal Year 2001, the division mailed out almost 34,000 letters to victims and concerned citizens who were registered on the notification database. The division also operates an **Automated Victim Notification Service** which allows victims and their families to obtain offender status information over the telephone at any time. The division operates a **Victim Impact Panel Program** to assist victims with recovery. Victim impact panels are composed of crime victims and survivors who are willing to share their victimization experiences with others. Participation on such panels often assists victims in their own recovery, as well as providing audience members with increased awareness and victim sensitivity. As a way of educating the public about the conditions of incarceration in Texas, the division conducts occasional **prison tours** for victims, their families, and members of the criminal justice system. The tour takes two half-days and includes visits to two prison units and to the execution chamber. The **Texas Crime Victim Clearinghouse** coordinates victim services and serves as a central information source about victim services and issues throughout the state. It produces a Victim Assistance Resource Directory and maintains statistics on victim impact statements. The **Victim Offender Mediation/Dialogue** (VOM/D) program is designed for victims of violent crime who request the opportunity to meet the offenders responsible for their victimization. Offenders must have admitted their guilt prior to the meeting, and participation in the mediation program is not included in the parole file. This ensures that offenders do not participate merely as a way of increasing their chances of receiving parole. The program provides victims with the opportunity to talk with the offender and ask questions, as well as giving offenders the opportunity to become responsible and accountable for their own behavior.[13]

Other Divisions

There are many other divisions within the TBCJ. The **Internal Audit Division** is responsible for assisting in the annual audit of the TDCJ. The results are reported directly to the TBCJ. In addition, the division reviews draft agency policies, serves on various agency committees, and provides various other types of assistance to management. The **Investigations Division** conducts inquiries into alleged misconduct by TDCJ employees. Current priorities include the investigation of allegations of the use of excessive or unnecessary force and into harassment of inmates who are engaged in legal activities. Both of these divisions are under the authority of the TBCJ's Office of the Inspector General.[14]

The **Programs and Services Division**, which was created in 1995, is responsible for coordinating activities among the various divisions of the Department. The division focuses on programs such as the Windham School District, the Substance Abuse Treatment Program, and the Sex Offender Treatment Program, which are implemented across divisions, to ensure that these programs are administered efficiently and consistently.[15] The **Office of the General Counsel** is the legal arm of the TDCJ and provides legal support and services to the Department. Duties include providing legal consultation to the Board, coordinating litigation activity, assisting in the preparation of Department policy, and assisting in any other legal matters. The Office also acts as a liaison between the Department and the Office of the State Attorney General, and between the Department and the courts.[16] The **Health Services Division** is responsible for ensuring that incarcerated offenders receive quality health care. The division monitors all health care delivery throughout the TDCJ.[17]

PRISON LABOR

The prison industries program in the TDCJ is known as **Texas Correctional Industries** (TCI). TCI provides a variety of products and services to the Department, to state government agencies, and to various local government agencies. This not only reduces Department costs, but provides offenders with job training and with opportunities for rehabilitation.[18]

TCI, which was originally known as the **Industrial Division** of the TDCJ, was established by the Prison Made Goods Act of 1963 and given the right to sell prison-made goods to tax-supported agencies and political subdivisions within the state of Texas. The purposes of TCI include:

> (1) provide work program participants with marketable job skills to help reduce recidivism through a coordinated program of:
> (A) job skills training;
> (B) documentation of work history; and
> (C) access to resources...; and
>
> (2) reduce department costs by providing products and articles for the department and providing products or articles for sale on a for-profit basis to the public or to agencies of the state or political subdivisions of the state.[19]

TCI has 45 facilities located in correctional institutions throughout Texas. The Garment Division includes garment, shoe, and mattress factories, and textile mills. These facilities manufacture work apparel, prisoner clothing, aprons, bedding (sheets, pillows, mattresses), and other textile items. The Graphic Division facilities manufacture a wide variety of signs, stickers, and other printed materials as well as license plates and janitorial supplies. The Division also includes a bindery and Braille facility and a box factory. Furniture Division facilities manufacture office, institutional, and modular furniture. Facilities in the Metal Division manufacture a wide variety of metal goods, including park equipment, metal signs, and stainless steel items. The Headquarters Division is responsible for the administration and day-to-day operation of the program. This includes developing marketing strategies for TCI, providing customer service, clerical support, human resources, and quality assurance programs.[20] In addition, TCI provides a variety of services, including furniture refinishing, school bus renovation, tire recapping, computer recovery (which involves refurbishing and updating computer equipment for use in Texas public schools), and GIS conversion.[21]

In addition to TCI, incarcerated offenders may be employed in a variety of other tasks. Inmates provide much of the prison support, working at jobs such as maintenance, laundry, cooking, and cleaning within the prison units. The prison system's agricultural program produces edible crops, livestock, and cotton. In addition, prison units that do not have enough arable land to participate in this program still run small farms or gardens and produce fresh vegetables which are donated to local food banks for distribution to low income families.

Low-risk offenders may be assigned to work outside prison units, supervised by armed correctional officers. Texas does not use chain gangs because only offenders on low-risk status are allowed to work outside. Offenders are involved in a number of community service programs. In FY 2002, offenders participated in 108 construction projects for Habitat for Humanity, contributing almost 72,000 hours of labor. Other community work projects involving inmates included clearing state land, cleaning state parks and beaches, renovating schools, and setting up baseball fields and playgrounds. During FY 2002, inmates participated in almost 4,000 such projects, contributing over 1.7 million work hours. This community service work by offenders saved the state approximately $9 million. In addition, inmates work with local food banks to sort, clean, and repackage food and other products for distribution to low income families throughout the state.[22]

LOCAL JAILS IN TEXAS

Local jails in Texas may be operated either by a county or by a municipality, or by a private agency under a vendor contract. In addition, state jail facilities are operated by the TDCJ. Jails have four primary functions:

- to book arrested suspects
- to house some defendants awaiting trial (those who were not granted pretrial release)

- to incarcerate convicted offenders who are sentenced to incarceration in a local facility

- *to hold inmates awaiting transfer to other facilities*

Jails in Texas are regulated by the **Texas Commission on Jail Standards**. The commission, which was created in 1975, establishes minimum standards for the construction, maintenance, and operation of jails (including the custody, care, and treatment of inmates), ensures that jails comply with these state-wide standards, and provides training and technical assistance in the areas of jail construction and management.[23]

There are over 250 local jails in Texas. As of January 1, 2004, the total population in local jails in Texas was 61,382. This figure includes inmates held in both county and contract facilities. The total jail capacity in the state is 79,697. Thus, overall, jails in Texas averaged 77 percent of capacity. Some jails in Texas are larger than prisons found in other states. For example, the **Harris County Jail System** has the capacity to house over 9,400 inmates.[24]

COMMUNITY SUPERVISION PROGRAMS IN TEXAS

In Texas, all offenders placed on some form of community-based supervision are supervised by divisions within the TDCJ. Those offenders on parole are supervised by the Parole Division, whereas offenders on community supervision (probation) are supervised by the Community Justice Assistance Division.

Community Supervision (Probation)

Texas began using **probation** in 1913, when certain non-violent offenders were allowed to serve their sentences in the community as an alternative to incarceration. The process was run locally until 1977, when the state legislature created the **Texas Adult Probation Commission** and gave it the task of creating and applying common probation standards statewide. In 1989, the Commission was merged with the Texas Department of Criminal Justice and became the **Community Justice Assistance Division**. The legislature also changed the name from probation to **community supervision**. Offenders placed on community supervision serve their sentences within the community, rather than in a prison or jail facility. Community supervision may be imposed for either felony or misdemeanor offenses. According to CCrP §42.12, Sec. 2(2):

> "Community supervision" means the placement of a defendant by a court under a continuum of programs and sanctions, with conditions imposed by the court for a specified period during which:
> (A) criminal proceedings are deferred without an adjudication of guilt; or
> (B) a sentence of imprisonment or confinement, imprisonment and fine, or confinement and fine, is probated and the imposition of sentence is suspended in whole or in part.

The CJAD supervises all community supervision services in Texas. The division works with the various community supervision and corrections departments throughout the state that supervise offenders. There are over 440,000 offenders on community supervision in Texas, including approximately 243,000 felony offenders and 200,000 misdemeanor offenders.[25] In 2001, Texas had the largest probation population in the United States.[26]

CJAD does not directly supervise offenders on community supervision. The Division works with local **Community Supervision and Corrections Departments** (CSCDs), which are responsible for the direct supervision and rehabilitation of offenders sentenced to community supervision. Currently, there are 121 CSCDs in Texas, serving all 254 counties. CSCDs are organized within local judicial districts and receive support from the district, as well as receiving funding from the CJAD. The local Departments are not part of the CJAD. CSCD employees work for the judicial district whereas CJAD employees work for the state of Texas. The Community Justice Assistance Division tracks CSCD performance, reviews budgets, distributes state funding, enforces mandatory standards of community supervision, and provides training and certification of community supervision officers.[27]

After being sentenced to community supervision, each offender is assigned a community supervision officer. This officer designs an individualized supervision program for the offender, which includes any conditions the court required at sentencing. CSCD officers have a variety of tools available to supervise and rehabilitate offenders and to protect the public. These include, but are not limited to:

- physical equipment, such as electronic monitoring and urinalysis testing
- special facilities such as local boot camps, restitution centers, day reporting centers, and residential treatment centers
- multiple levels of supervision such as basic supervision and intensive supervision
- specialized caseloads targeting sex offenders, substance abusers, or offenders with special needs (e.g., mentally or physically disabled offenders)
- rehabilitation programs, including continuing education, vocational training, cognitive skills training, life skills training, and substance abuse treatment
- victim notification program to provide information and support to victims of offenders on community supervision.

In some cases, the court may require an offender to live in a residential facility while on community supervision. This provides a higher level of supervision but does not use up scarce prison space on non-violent offenders. There are several types of residential facilities for offenders on community supervision, including boot camps, restitution centers, court residential treatment centers, substance abuse treatment facilities, and intermediate sanctions facilities.

Boot camps, which resemble a military basic training program, focus on young, first-time offenders. In addition to strict supervision, discipline, and physical exercise, they provide general education, life skills training, and substance abuse education, and require offenders to make restitution both to their victims and to society. Offenders who have been ordered to pay restitution may be required to live in a **restitution center** if they have difficulty keeping a job or paying restitution, or if they have substance abuse problems. Offenders living in these centers must get and keep a full-time job, perform community service restitution (essentially volunteer work in the community), and attend education and life skills training classes.

Offenders with drug or alcohol problems may be assigned to a **court residential treatment center** to receive treatment. These centers also provide education and life skills training and may also offer vocational and employment assistance. **Substance abuse treatment facilities** also provide treatment and rehabilitation of offenders with drug or alcohol problems. Finally, offenders who violate court-ordered conditions of community supervision may be sent to an **intermediate sanctions facility** rather than having his or her supervision revoked and sending him/her to prison.[28]

Parole

Unlike probation, **parole** is not a sentence. It is a form of conditional early release from a sentence of incarceration. The offender serves a portion of his or her sentence under supervision in the community. The offender is released from the custody of the TDCJ Institutional Division and serves the remainder of his or her sentence under the control and supervision of the TDJC **Parole Division.**[29] The offender must report to a parole officer on a regular schedule and must obey specified conditions of release until the sentence is completed.

The TDCJ Parole Division

The Parole Division of the TDCJ is responsible for supervising offenders who have served time in a prison and who are now completing their sentences in the community. The Division is not responsible for deciding who is released, for assigning release conditions, or for revoking parole; these decisions are the responsibility of the Board of Pardons and Paroles. However, the Division does assist the board by providing them with information necessary to make these determinations.

In addition to supervising offenders in the community, the Division has a number of pre-release functions, including investigation of parole plans proposed by incarcerated offenders and tracking cases eligible for parole and submitting them to the Board of Pardons and Paroles. The Division also supervises inmates who are participating in two pre-release programs. The **Pre-Parole Transfer Program** provides inmates who are within one year of their parole or mandatory supervision release date with counseling, substance abuse education, and life skills, academic, and vocational training. Participants may be transferred to a secure community-based pre-parole facility while in this program. The program may allow pre-parolees to engage in job interviews and arrange for employment in the community after their release. The **Work Program** is designed for inmates who are between six months and two years of parole eligibility and allows them to live in a secure facility while employed in on-site private industry programs. Participants receive either minimum wage or the prevailing wage for similar work in the location of the facility and must contribute up to 80 percent of their wages to cover the costs of supervision and housing, pay victim restitution and dependant support, and maintain a savings account.[30]

The Texas Board of Pardons and Paroles

The **Texas Board of Pardons and Paroles** (BPP) is the agency responsible for determining whether eligible inmates are released into the community under some type of parole supervision. The BPP also determines the conditions of release for each offender and responds to any violations of those conditions. In addition, the BPP makes recommendations to the governor on executive clemency matters (pardons, reprieves, and commutations).[31]

The BPP is composed of 18 members who are appointed by the governor, with the advice and consent of the Senate, and who serve six-year terms. To be eligible to serve on the Board, a prospective member must be representative of the general public, be a resident citizen of Texas, and have been a resident in the state for at least two years prior to appointment.[32]

Types of Parole Release

There are four ways in which an offender may be released from the Institutional Division. They may be paroled, released on mandatory supervision, released on discretionary mandatory supervision, or discharged after serving their entire term of incarceration. Any offender who is released prior to completing his or her entire sentence becomes the responsibility of the Parole Division.[33]

Offenders who are on **mandatory supervision** are released from prison when their calendar time served and their good time credit equals the length of the sentenced prison term (their "minimum expiration date.") The BPP does not have to approve the release of these inmates, although it is responsible for setting the mandatory conditions they must follow upon release.

Until 1996, mandatory supervision release was automatic. All offenders who are incarcerated for offenses committed prior to September 1, 1996, and who are eligible for mandatory supervision, must be released upon reaching their minimum expiration date. However, in 1995, the state legislature gave the BBP the authority to review and approve for release on **discretionary mandatory supervision** all offenders incarcerated for offenses committed on or after September 1, 1996. The BPP has the right to either grant or deny release for these offenders.

Finally, **parole** involves the release of an offender upon the approval of the BPP. Parole release is discretionary and always involves a decision by the Board. An offender's initial parole eligibility date may occur well before his or her mandatory supervision date. However, the BPP is not required to approve parole at any parole review hearing. Parolees include offenders released on Medically Recommended Intensive Supervision (MRIS). MRIS candidates include non-violent offenders who are mentally or terminally ill, physically handicapped, or mentally retarded. They must be judged by the BPP to pose no threat to the public safety.[34]

Regardless of the type of release, all offenders must report to a parole officer on a regular schedule, must obey specified rules and conditions of release (and be subject to arrest and re-incarceration for violation of these conditions), and must remain in the custody of the state until sentence is completed. All categories of releasees are supervised by the Parole Division.

As of August 31, 2002, 78,118 active releasees were being supervised by the Parole Division. The majority of these (over 81 percent) were on regular supervision. Approximately 14 percent required specialized supervision (these included sex offenders, substance abuse cases, and offenders with special needs), 3 percent were assigned to intensive supervision and/or electronic monitoring, and 2 percent to super-intensive supervision.[35]

The Process of Release and Supervision

Several months before reaching his or her parole eligibility review date, an offender will be interviewed by a parole officer, who prepares a case summary. This document includes the facts of the case, the offender's disciplinary record in prison, his or her physical and mental conditions, any other relevant information (e.g., assaultive behavior), and a summary of positive and negative factors. The offender provides the parole officer with the release plan, which includes information where the offender will live upon release, any prospective employment, and any other plans (e.g., drug/alcohol treatment).

The offender's case is then reviewed by a BPP parole panel. One or more members of the panel may interview the offender prior to the panel, but this is at the discretion of the individual members. In most cases, the panel consists of three BBP members; a majority vote is required for parole to be granted. However, certain categories of offenders may only be granted parole upon a two-thirds majority vote of the entire BPP. These include capital felons, persons convicted of aggravated assault, and persons convicted of indecency with a child. The BPP is never required to grant release.

All offenders released on parole or mandatory supervision are required to obey certain rules of release and may have their release revoked for violation of these rules. Rules of release include (but are not limited to):

- report regularly to an assigned parole officer
- obey all local, county, state, and federal laws
- obtain written permission from the parole officer before changing residence or leaving the state

- do not own, possess, sell, or control any firearm or other prohibited or illegal weapon, do not unlawfully carry any weapon, and do not use, attempt to use, or threaten to use any object to injure or attempt to injure another person

- do not associate with persons of criminal background or with any person or group prohibited by written instruction of the parole officer

- do not enter into agreements to act as informer or special agent for any law enforcement agent without specific written approval of the Parole Division

- abide by any special conditions of release imposed by the DPP

Special or discretionary release conditions that may be imposed by the BPP may include (but are not limited to):

- halfway house placement
- intensive supervision
- electronic monitoring
- drug monitoring (e.g., urinalysis)
- mandatory participation in substance abuse treatment programs, psychological counseling, or educational programs

The BPP may also require violent offenders to participate in a **Super-Intensive Supervision Program** (SISP) as a special condition of release. This program, which was mandated by the state legislature in 1997 in GC §508.317, provides a higher level of supervision for potentially dangerous offenders as a way of protecting the public safety. All offenders released into SISP are supervised through some type of electronic monitoring and must comply with 24-hour schedules that are pre-approved by a parole officer in writing. Offenders meeting one or more of the following criteria are considered for SISP placement:

- a current or past conviction for a violent offense
- a current or past conviction for an attempted violent offense
- a current or past conviction (including juvenile convictions) for any offense that involved the threat of violence that could result in bodily injury

SISP parole officers undergo specialized training and have smaller caseloads (generally 14 to 20 offenders per officer). Releasees placed in SISP have a minimum of ten in-person contacts with parole officers each month. All SISP offenders are electronically monitored. All technical violations are dealt with severely, rather than by the system of graduated sanctions employed for regular parolees.

Electronic Monitoring of Parolees

Electronic monitoring allows additional supervision of releasees. It is used primarily for those releasees requiring a higher level of supervision, including, but not limited to, those on SISP. It may also be used for offenders on community supervision. Texas began using electronic monitoring in 1987. Currently there are three types of electronic monitoring systems in use in the state. **Continuous electronic monitoring** requires the offender to wear a radio transmitter around his/her ankle and to have a receiving unit attached to a telephone line in his or her home. If the releasee moves more than a specified distance from the receiving unit, a central monitoring station notifies a parole officer of the violation. **Drive-by electronic monitoring** also requires the offender to wear the ankle transmitter. However, the releasee is monitored by the parole officer using a portable receiver; this allows surveillance when the releasee is not actually at home. Finally, **video monitoring** requires the releasee to telephone the central monitoring station from a designated telephone at scheduled and random times during the day. A computer uses a sample of the releasee's voice to determine if the caller matches the sample. Violations occur if the voice of the caller does not match the sample, if the releasee fails to call in at the scheduled time, or if he or she does not call from the designated location.

BECOMING A CORRECTIONAL OFFICER

To become a correctional officer in Texas, applicants must meet certain minimum eligibility criteria. These include:

- be a U.S. citizen or alien authorized to work in the U.S.
- minimum age of 18
- high school diploma from a state-accredited school or state-issued GED
- not be on active military duty
- no convictions for any felony, drug-related offense, or offense involving domestic violence
- no Class A or B misdemeanor convictions in the last 5 years
- not be on probation for any criminal offense
- no criminal charges pending and no outstanding warrants
- be registered with Selective Service if applicable
- be able to perform all essential functions of a correctional officer, with or without reasonable accommodation[36]

Applicants who meet these criteria must pass a TDCJ pre-employment test, a TDCJ drug test, and a background screening. If selected by the TDCJ, applicants go through a training program at the TDCJ Correctional Officer Training Academy in Beeville or at one of the other academies located around the state. Trainees attending the Beeville and Gatesville academies receive free room and board. Training includes approximately 200 hours of instruction over six weeks. It includes training in firearms, self defense, chemical agents, first aid and CPR, physical training, non-violent crisis intervention, and standards for use of force. After completing academy training, the trainees participate in two weeks of on-the-job training at the unit to which they are assigned.

The basic eligibility criteria for parole caseworkers are similar but not identical. They include:

- be a U.S. citizen or alien authorized to work in the U.S.
- minimum age of 18
- bachelor's degree from an institution of higher education accredited by the Council for Higher Education (preferred majors include criminal justice, counseling, social work, psychology, and sociology)
- experience in casework, or case processing in criminal justice or social services is preferred
- not be on active military duty
- no convictions for domestic violence
- not be on probation for any criminal offense
- no criminal charges pending and no outstanding warrants
- at least 15 years since the completion of any sentence (including probation) for a felony conviction
- be registered with Selective Service if applicable
- be able to perform all essential functions of a parole officer or caseworker, with or without reasonable accommodation[37]

Applicants must submit to mandatory drug testing and a background check. Applicants who are hired first go through an on-the-job training program in their region and then enter the TDCJ Parole Caseworker Training Academy in Beeville. The academy consists of three weeks of instruction and training. Caseworkers must have at least one year of full-time wage-earning employment in casework or case processing to advance to the position of parole officer.

NOTES

1. GC §492.002
2. GC §493.001
3. Texas Department of Criminal Justice - Correctional Institutions Division (http://www.tdcj.state.tx.us/cid/cid_home.htm)
4. Texas Department of Criminal Justice (2003). *Statistical Report: Fiscal Year 2002*. Available online at: http://www.tdcj.state.tx.us/publications/publications-home.htm
5. *Ibid*
6. Texas Department of Criminal Justice - Correctional Institutions Division, *op cit.*
7. Windham School District (2002). *Annual Performance Report: 2001-2002*. Available online at: http://www.windhamschooldistrict.org/apr.pdf
8. Texas Department of Criminal Justice - Correctional Institutions Division, *op cit.*
9. *Ibid*

10. Texas Department of Criminal Justice (2003). *Statistical Report: Fiscal Year 2002, op cit.*
11. Texas Department of Criminal Justice - Community Justice Assistance Division (http://www.tdcj.state.tx.us/cjad/cjad-home.htm)
12. Texas Department of Criminal Justice - Parole Division (http://www.tdcj.state.tx.us/parole/parole-home.htm)
13. Texas Department of Criminal Justice - Victim Services Division (http://www.tdcj.state.tx.us/victim/victim-home.htm)
14. Texas Department of Criminal Justice - Office of the Inspector General (http://www.tdcj.state.tx.us/inspector.general/inspector.gnl-home.htm)
15. Texas Department of Criminal Justice - Programs and Services Division (http://www.tdcj.state.tx.us/pgm&svcs/pgms&svcs-home.htm)
16. Texas Department of Criminal Justice - Office of the General Counsel (http://www.tdcj.state.tx.us/ogc/ogc-home.htm)
17. Texas Department of Criminal Justice - Health Services Division (http://www.tdcj.state.tx.us/health/health-home.htm)
18. Texas Correctional Industries web site (http://www.tci.tdcj.state.tx.us/)
19. GC §497.002(a)
20. Texas Correctional Industries recruitment brochure (http://www.tdcj.state.tx.us/publications/tci/TCI-brochure-2003.PDF)
21. Texas Correctional Industries web site, *op cit.*
22. Texas Department of Criminal Justice (2003). *Statistical Summary: Fiscal Year 2002*. Available online at: http://www.tdcj.state.tx.us/publications/publications-home.htm
23. Texas Commission on Jail Standards home page (http://www.tcjs.state.tx.us/)
24. Texas Commission on Jail Standards - Jail Population Report, January 1, 2004 (http://www.tcjs.state.tx.us/jailpop.html)
25. Texas Department of Criminal Justice - Community Justice Assistance Division, *op cit.*
26. Texas Department of Criminal Justice (2003). *Community Supervision in Texas: Summary Statistics, January 2003* (http://www.tdcj.state.tx.us/publications/cjad/cjad-publications-home.htm)
27. Texas Department of Criminal Justice - Community Justice Assistance Division, *op cit.*
28. *Ibid*
29. GC §508.001(6)
30. Texas Department of Criminal Justice - Parole Division, *op cit.*
31. Texas Constitution, Article IV, Section 11
32. Texas Board of Pardons and Paroles home page (http://www.tdcj.state.tx.us/bpp/)
33. Texas Board of Pardons and Paroles (2002). *2002 Annual Report*. (http://www.tdcj.state.tx.us/bpp/publications/publications.html)
34. Texas Department of Criminal Justice - Parole Division, *op cit.*
35. Texas Department of Criminal Justice (2003). *Statistical Summary: Fiscal Year 2002 op cit.*
36. Texas Department of Criminal Justice - employment information (http://www.tdcj.state.tx.us/vacancy/)
37. *Ibid*

CHAPTER 9

THE JUVENILE JUSTICE SYSTEM IN TEXAS

INTRODUCTION

The definition of a **juvenile** in Texas is similar to that of many other states. Family Code (FC) §51.02(2) states that a:

> "Child" means a person who is:
> (A) ten years of age or older and under 17 years of age; or
> (B) seventeen years of age or older and under 18 years of age who is alleged or found to have engaged in delinquent conduct or conduct indicating a need for supervision as a result of acts committed before becoming 17 years of age.

FC §51.03.(a) defines **delinquent conduct** as

> (1) conduct, other than a traffic offense, that violates a penal law of this state or of the United States punishable by imprisonment or by confinement in jail;
> (2) conduct that violates a lawful order of a municipal court or justice court under circumstances that would constitute contempt of that court;
> (3) conduct that violates Section 49.04, 49.05, 49.06, 49.07, or 49.08, Penal Code; or
> (4) conduct that violates Section 106.041, Alcoholic Beverage Code, relating to driving under the influence of alcohol by a minor (third or subsequent offense).

Texas also recognizes the concept of **status offender**, which is defined in FC §51.02(15) as:

> a child who is accused, adjudicated, or convicted for conduct that would not, under state law, be a crime if committed by an adult, including:
> (A) truancy...;
> (B) running away from home...;
> (C) a fineable only offense under Section 51.03(b)(1) transferred to the juvenile court under Section 51.08(b), but only if the conduct constituting the offense would not have been criminal if engaged in by an adult;
> (D) failure to attend school...;
> (E) a violation of standards of student conduct...;
> (F) a violation of a juvenile curfew ordinance or order;
> (G) a violation of a provision of the Alcoholic Beverage Code applicable to minors only; or

(H) a violation of any other fineable only offense under Section 8.07(a)(4) or (5), Penal Code, but only if the conduct constituting the offense would not have been criminal if engaged in by an adult.

THE HISTORY OF JUVENILE JUSTICE IN TEXAS

The state of Texas has treated juveniles different from adult offenders since the mid-1850s, when the state legislature passed a law exempting juveniles who were under the age of 13 from criminal prosecution in certain situations. The legislature also authorized the construction of a separate correctional facility to house juveniles. Although construction was delayed by the outbreak of the Civil War, the **Gatesville State School for Boys** was opened in 1889, and the **Gainesville State School** (for girls) opened in 1916. Until 1920, all state facilities for juveniles were independently run and reported to the state governor. Between 1920 and 1949, these facilities were run by the **Texas Board of Control.**

In 1949, the state legislature created the **Texas Youth Development Council**, which coordinated efforts to develop community-based youth services and administered juvenile training schools in Texas. In 1957, administration of all state juvenile training schools and all homes for neglected and dependent children was handed over to the **Texas Youth Council**. In 1961, this agency also began providing parole services for delinquent youth. During the 1960s and the 1970s, juvenile justice services in Texas focused attention on the development of community-based alternatives to institutional delivery of services. A county juvenile probation subsidy program was created, which was eventually made the responsibility of the **Texas Juvenile Probation Commission**, created in 1981. Several landmark Texas and U.S. Supreme Court cases eventually led the Texas Legislature to enact Title 3 of the Texas Family Code in 1973. This section is now known as the **Juvenile Justice Code**.

In 1983, the Texas Youth Council was renamed the **Texas Youth Commission** (TYC). In the mid-1980s, Texas experienced a sharp increase in the rate of juvenile crime in the state. Between 1988 and 1993, referrals to juvenile probation for delinquent activity increased 61 percent while referrals for violent offenses increased 161 percent. The rate of homicides in Texas rose to 12.8 per 100,000, almost twice the national rate of 6.6 per 100,000. In addition, there was a 285 percent increase in the number of juveniles committed to the TYC for violent crimes.

In 1987, in response to this increase in violent juvenile crime, Texas adopted **blended sentencing**. This technique combines a criminal sentence and a traditional juvenile court disposition, allowing juveniles who are given determinate sentences to serve the first part of the sentence in TYC and later be transferred to the adult system to complete the sentence.

During the 1990s, juvenile crime in Texas continued to increase. Between 1990 and 1998, the proportion of total arrested suspects in Texas who were juveniles increased from 23 percent to 35 percent. In addition, arrests for juvenile violent crime increased. TYC commitments increased along with the increased rate of juvenile crime. In fiscal year 1993, there were 1,564 new commitments; this number increased 104 percent by fiscal year 1998, when there were 3,188 new commitments to TYC.

In 1995, the Texas Legislature passed juvenile reform legislation emphasizing the "get tough, balanced approach" which combined punishment with rehabilitation for juvenile offenders. Elements of this legislation, which became effective in January, 1996, included:

- adding the concept of "punishment" as a purpose of the Juvenile Justice Code

- reducing the certification age to 14 (from 15) for capital felonies and first degree felonies; once a juvenile is certified, he/she will automatically be transferred to adult criminal court for all subsequent felony offenses

- expansion of determinate sentencing – eleven new offenses (all violent crimes against persons) were added to the original five

- increasing the range of possible sentences to a maximum of 40 years for first degree felonies and establishing minimum confinement periods for sentenced juvenile offenders

- authorizing TYC to request that the juvenile court transfer sentenced juveniles after age 16 to adult prison for completion of sentence

- requiring all sentenced youth to complete sentences after age 21 (in some cases age 19) on adult parole

- requiring all referrals to juvenile court for felonies and misdemeanors involving violence or weapons to be reviewed by the prosecuting attorney for possible prosecution

In the late 1990s and the start of the 21st century, juvenile crime rates began to level off and commitments to TYC showed a slight decline.[1]

THE TEXAS JUVENILE JUSTICE SYSTEM TODAY

The **Texas Juvenile Justice System** includes elements at both the state and local levels, each with specific functions and responsibilities.

State Agencies

There are two main agencies at the state level which deal with juvenile justice. The **Texas Youth Commission** (TYC), which was originally created in 1949 as the Texas Youth Development Council, is responsible for all juvenile correctional institutions throughout Texas, providing care, custody, and rehabilitation for violent and chronic juvenile offenders who are committed to secure custody. The **Texas Juvenile Probation Commission** (TJPC) was created in 1981 and is responsible for coordinating all juvenile probation services throughout the state, setting and maintaining minimum state standards, and ensuring that effective probation services are available to juveniles throughout Texas. These agencies are discussed in more detail later in this chapter.

There are several other state agencies which are involved in the juvenile justice system. The **Texas Department of Mental Health and Mental Retardation** provides services to juveniles who are mentally ill or mentally retarded and who either are found to be not competent to stand trial or found not responsible for their conduct. The **Texas Department of Protective and Regulatory Services** is responsible for providing a variety of services to neglected and abused children, and to at-risk children and their families. The **Texas Department of Public Safety** operates the Juvenile Justice Information System, a state-wide computer database collecting information regarding the arrest, adjudication, and disposition of juvenile offenders.

Local Agencies

There are a large number of local-level agencies which are heavily involved in the juvenile justice system. Each county in Texas has a **County Juvenile Board** which oversees the juvenile justice system at the local level. Some boards cover multiple counties. Members of the board generally include all district court judges, county court judges, and statutory court judges. The board hires the Chief Juvenile Probation Officer for the county and is responsible for making budget and policy decisions for the county's juvenile probation department. The juvenile board also selects the **juvenile court judges**. Currently, there are over 400 juvenile court judges in Texas. The **County Juvenile Probation Department** deals with approximately 97 percent of all juveniles who commit crimes. Only about 3 percent of juvenile offenders are sentenced to a TYC facility. There are 168 juvenile probation departments in Texas.[2]

The **County Commissioner's Court** provides funding to the juvenile justice system. Each county also has a **Juvenile Prosecutor** or **Juvenile Prosecuting Attorney**, who is usually an Assistant District Attorney or Assistant County Attorney (depending on local preference). **Justice** and **Municipal Court Judges** are heavily involved in the juvenile justice system because they handle most Class C misdemeanors and ordinance violations committed by juveniles, as well as cases such as truancy and failure to attend school. When juvenile court judges are unavailable, justice and municipal court judges will frequently magistrate juvenile offenders (the procedural equivalent of Miranda warnings) and conduct detention hearings. **Local law enforcement officers** investigate criminal offenses by juveniles and arrest juvenile offenders. Finally, **volunteers** are used in many counties in areas such as mediation, victim-offender programs, mentoring, restitution, and prevention programs.[3]

WHAT HAPPENS TO A JUVENILE WHO BREAKS THE LAW IN TEXAS?

A juvenile who breaks the law in Texas enters the Texas **juvenile justice system**. This system differs in several key ways from the adult criminal justice system. If the police catch a juvenile engaged in a minor violation of the law, the officer may choose to simply warn the child and his or her parents. If the crime is more serious, or if additional action is required to protect either the child or the public, or to prevent future offenses, the case will be forwarded to local juvenile probation officials. All juveniles arrested for an alleged delinquent offense which, if committed by an adult would be punishable by incarceration in a jail or prison are fingerprinted and their criminal history record entered into a statewide central information database.

The juvenile is then taken to the local **juvenile probation intake unit** where s/he goes through an intake process and is evaluated by an intake officer. Some cases may be resolved by counseling, others through referrals to other social agencies. In those cases where charges will be filed in court, the intake officer must decide where the juvenile will stay while awaiting judicial proceedings. Most are released to a parent or guardian but some are held in secure juvenile detention or in a shelter. Juvenile detention centers are operated by local juvenile probation departments or by private companies under contract. Their function is to protect both the juvenile and the community and to ensure that the juvenile appears in court.[4]

During 2002, a total of 140,085 juveniles between the ages of 10 and 17 were arrested by police in Texas. Of these, 81,225 (58 percent) were referred to juvenile probation departments. The remainder were warned and released, diverted (frequently into some type of deferred prosecution program), or handled in justice and municipal courts. An additional 24,685 cases were referred by other sources, including parents, schools, the TYC, and various social service agencies. The majority of those cases referred to juvenile probation departments were not sent to the juvenile court.[5]

At the intake process, a determination is made whether or not to detain the juvenile. The Texas Family Code requires that a juvenile must be released to a suitable parent or guardian unless one of the following five statutory criteria are present:

(1) he is likely to abscond or be removed from the jurisdiction of the court;
(2) suitable supervision, care, or protection for him is not being provided by a parent, guardian, custodian, or other person;
(3) he has no parent, guardian, custodian, or other person able to return him to the court when required;
(4) he may be dangerous to himself or may threaten the safety of the public if released; or

(5) he has previously been found to be a delinquent child or has previously been convicted of a penal offense punishable by a term in jail or prison and is likely to commit an offense if released.[6]

The intake detention decision is usually made by a juvenile probation officer. If the juvenile is detained at intake, a judge must make a finding of probable cause within 48 hours and must hold a **detention hearing** within one to two working days. The same criteria used at intake are also considered at the detention hearing to decide if the juvenile will be detained until adjudication. In 2002, almost 50,000 juveniles were held in secure detention prior to adjudication hearings. Of these, approximately 30 percent were released in less than one day.[7]

After charges are filed and while the juvenile is waiting to go to court, a probation officer begins a court investigation. This includes an assessment of the juvenile's behavior at home, at school, and in social relationships. The probation officer prepares a report to help the judge in making his or her decision. In some cases, generally those involving younger offenders who committed less serious offenses, the juvenile will be diverted into a **deferred prosecution** program. This six-month program allows juveniles to avoid going through the adjudication process and limits their involvement with the formal juvenile justice system.[8]

The court proceeding is known as an **adjudication hearing** The juvenile, his or her attorney, and members of the juvenile's family appear before a judge or jury. Unlike some states, in Texas a juvenile has the right to a trial by jury unless the juvenile and his or her attorney waive that right. The jury verdict must be unanimous and, in determinate sentencing cases, there must be twelve jurors. The majority of juvenile cases in 2002 were disposed of by juvenile probation departments or resolved by juvenile prosecutors. Approximately 43 percent were resolved by the juvenile court.[9]

If the judge or jury determines that the juvenile committed a delinquent act, or some conduct that indicates a need for supervision, the juvenile is adjudicated for the offense and the judge will order a **disposition hearing** to determine disposition. There is no right to a jury in this stage, except in determinate sentencing cases. At the disposition hearing, the judge has a variety of options, ranging from dismissal of the case to long-term confinement. There are several basic dispositions used in juvenile court. If the juvenile committed a felony offense and is at least 14 years of age, the judge has the option of **certifying** the juvenile to stand trial in an adult criminal court. Juveniles who committed serious offenses may fall under the **Determinate Sentencing Law**, which allows the court to confine the juvenile for up to 40 years, first in a TYC facility and then later possibly in an adult institution. If the juvenile committed a less serious offense but still requires some type of confinement, the judge may order the juvenile committed to the TYC for an indeterminate period of time, although the juvenile will be automatically discharged upon reaching the age of 21. Finally, in most cases, the judge will place the juvenile on some type of probation involving supervision in the community or in a residential treatment facility.[10]

JUVENILE PROBATION IN TEXAS

Juvenile probation in Texas is provided at the local and/or county level, by the 168 local juvenile probation departments. The **Texas Juvenile Probation Commission** collaborates with these local departments, providing funding and training, setting and enforcing minimum standards, and collecting, analyzing, and distributing relevant data.[10]

Local juvenile probation departments handle approximately 97 percent of all juveniles who commit crimes in the state. Certification as a juvenile probation officer requires a bachelor's degree and one year of graduate study or one year of related work experience as well as 40 hours of basic probation training. Each department is headed by a **Chief Juvenile Probation Officer** who is chosen by, and reports to, the County Juvenile Board. The Chief Juvenile Probation Officer is responsible for the daily operations of the county probation department. In smaller counties, he or she may also directly supervise probationers.

Each year, over 100,000 youth between the ages of 10 and 17 are referred to county juvenile probation departments. If the violation is minor, the police may choose to give the child and his or her parents a warning. If the crime is more serious, the case will be forwarded to county probation officials for review. Many cases are resolved through referrals, counseling, and other diversion techniques. If the district attorney does file charges against the juvenile, the probation officer assigned to the case will assess the juvenile's situation and report his or her findings to the judge. In most cases, if the juvenile is adjudicated delinquent, the judge will order the youth placed either on probation supervision within the community or in a private residential treatment facility.[10]

Juvenile Probation Services in Dallas County

Dallas County Probation Services includes four main units. **Field Probation Services** employs 85 probation officers and has ten district offices. After a petition has been filed on a juvenile, s/he becomes the responsibility of this unit. Juveniles who are referred to the Probation Services Department may be detained in a secure facility prior to adjudication or released to a parent or guardian. Many of those released prior to adjudication are placed on **pre-adjudicated intensive supervision** and supervised by a field probation officer. Prior to the adjudication hearing, probation officers in the Field Probation Services Unit conduct an investigation of the child and his or her family and present recommendations and an intervention plan to the court for consideration. Because the most common disposition made by the juvenile court is probation in the home, the majority of adjudicated juveniles remain the responsibility of Field Probation Services until the expiration of probation. During 2002, over 3,600 juveniles were supervised on formal probation by this unit.[11]

The **Intake/Detention Screening Unit** is responsible for all juveniles who are referred to the Dallas County Juvenile Detention Center. The Unit has two main functions: determining which juveniles should be processed by the court and which should be considered for deferred services, and determining which juveniles are eligible for pre-adjudication release. During 2002, the staff of the unit screened 5,710 juveniles. Of these approximately 55 percent were held for detention hearings.[12]

The **Assessment Unit** conducts the assessments of pre-adjudicated juveniles who have petitions pending. The staff of this unit conduct interviews with the juvenile, his or her family, school officials, victims, and the police. This information is used to develop dispositional recommendations for the juvenile court. The Unit also prepares reports for certification hearings on any child that the District Attorney's Office is trying to certify to stand trial as an adult. During 2002, the Unit received 1,162 cases and completed 1,037 predisposition reports as well as 24 adult certification reports.[13]

Staff members of the **Court Liaison Unit** appear in court on behalf of the field probation officer. They also meet with juveniles and their parents or guardians to ensure that they understand the various judicial proceedings, including any possible terms and conditions of probation that may have been ordered by the court. During 2002, the unit represented 7,940 cases in court.[14]

THE TEXAS YOUTH COMMISSION

The **Texas Youth Commission** (TYC) is the juvenile corrections agency for the state of Texas. It was originally created in 1949 as the Texas Youth Development Council; the name was changed to the **Texas Youth Council** in 1957, and it was renamed the TYC in 1983. The TYC is responsible for the custody and rehabilitation of serious and chronic delinquents in the state. Crimes committed by youth sent to TYC include murder, rape, assault, robbery, burglary, and drug offenses.

Most juveniles committed to the TYC committed felony offenses when they were between the ages of ten and 17. The Commission has the option of maintaining jurisdiction over juvenile offenders until they reach age 21. In FY 2003, there were 2,511 new commitments to TYC. Of these, approximately 90 percent were male and 10 percent female. Approximately 25 percent were white, 31 percent were black, and 44 percent were Hispanic. The most common offenses for which the youths were committed were burglary (22 percent), unlawful use of a motor vehicle (10 percent) and drug offenses (9 percent).[15] The population of juveniles under supervision by TYC has been declining in recent years. The residential population peaked in 2002, with 5,646 juveniles. At the end of 2003, this figure had decreased to 4,825.[16]

The majority of juveniles sent to TYC are assigned to one of the fifteen **secure correctional facilities** operated by TYC. The remainder are placed in **contract facilities** run by local governments and private sector providers. These include both residential facilities and non-residential programs and services. In addition, TYC operates nine **halfway houses**. After spending time in a secure facility, some juveniles are placed in a community-based halfway house as a transition back to the community.

Only approximately three percent of all juveniles referred to county juvenile probation departments are actually committed to the TYC. These are generally violent or chronic offenders. There are two ways in which juveniles may be committed to the TYC:

1. Juveniles who have committed extremely serious offenses may have been sentenced under Texas' Determinate Sentencing Law. This permits incarceration

for up to 40 years. The sentence may be served first at TYC, with an optional court transfer to prison at a later date, depending on the juvenile's behavior.

2. Juveniles who have not received a determinate sentence may be sent to TYC for an indeterminate period. The amount of time is determined by TYC but offenders may remain in TYC custody only until they reach the age of 21. This is the most common situation.

Although juveniles who are not committed to TYC under the Determinate Sentencing Law are assigned a minimum length of stay, this is merely the minimum time that they must spend in a residential program before being considered for parole. Juveniles are required to earn parole by showing progress in both rehabilitation and education programs and may stay well past their minimum length of stay. The average length of stay in a residential facility has increased significantly in recent years. In FY 1995, the average length of stay was 9.1 months but by FY 2002, it had increased to a high of 22.7 months. In FY 2003, the average length of stay decreased slightly, to 22.3 months.[17]

The minimum length of stay is determined by TYC, based on the juvenile's security classification. Juveniles without a determinate sentence (i.e., with an indeterminate sentence) may be classified as follows:

- **Type A Violent Offender**: a juvenile classified for committing or attempting to commit capital murder, murder, aggravated sexual assault, or sexual assault.

- **Type B Violent Offender**: a juvenile classified for committing or attempting to commit criminally negligent homicide, manslaughter, kidnapping, unlawful restraint, felony or aggravated assault, indecency with a child, injury to a child, elderly or disabled person, child abandonment or endangerment, felony deadly conduct, felony aiding suicide, first- or second-degree tampering with a consumer product, arson, robbery or aggravated robbery, burglary with intent to commit a violent offense, intoxication assault or manslaughter, participating in a riot at a TYC facility, or assault with bodily injury to TYC staff.

- **Chronic Serious Offender**: a juvenile who has been adjudicated on at least three separate occasions for committing a felony.

- ***Controlled Substance Dealer***: a juvenile classified for felony-level drug manufacturing or delivery.

- **Firearms Offender**: a juvenile who had a firearm during the offense for which s/he has been classified.

- **General Offender**: includes all other juveniles, most of whom were assigned to TYC for non-violent or property crimes.

The minimum length of stay for Type A violent offenders is 24 months. The minimum length of stay for Type B violent offenders, chronic serious offenders, controlled substance dealers, and firearms offenders is 12 months. The minimum length of stay for general offenders is 9 months.[18]

All juveniles committed to TYC are first sent to the **Marlin Orientation and Assessment Center** where they undergo a medical examination, psychological evaluation, education assessment, social summary, a needs assessment to determine requirements for specialized treatment, and an orientation to the TYC program and expectations. These evaluations and tests are used to determine where the juvenile will be placed. Most youth spend approximately two months at Marlin.

Most juveniles generally spend most of their minimum length of stay in a secure residential facility. As they near the end of this period, they may be moved to a halfway house or residential contract program, or may remain in the secure facility until release on parole. Juveniles placed on parole receive supervision from a parole officer. A juvenile who performs well while on parole will be discharged from the TYC. In addition, TYC authority ends when the juvenile reaches the age of 21; at this point, discharge is automatic. Juveniles who commit additional criminal offenses while under TYC jurisdiction may be charged as adults. Juveniles with a determinate sentence will be assigned to a secure residential facility and may be transferred to the Texas Department of Criminal Justice at a later date.

TYC rehabilitation is based on a concept known as **resocialization**, which focuses on correctional therapy, education, work, and discipline training. Juveniles spend 16 hours a day involved in various resocialization activities. These are divided into phases through which each juvenile may move through at his/her own pace; he/she must show specific competencies in each phase before moving on to the next. Basic needs such as food, clothing, shelter, medical care, and due process are provided to all juveniles in TYC custody. However, juveniles earn privileges and rewards by completing resocialization phases and complying with TYC program rules.

In addition to resocialization, TYC provides specialized intensive treatment for juveniles with identified special needs. These programs include those designed for capital offenders, sex offenders, juveniles with chemical dependencies, severely emotionally disturbed juveniles, and mentally retarded juveniles. The assessment process at the Marlin Center is designed to identify juveniles who will most benefit from specialized treatment and to place them in the appropriate program.[19]

JUVENILE PAROLE IN TEXAS

The TYC is also responsible for supervising juveniles who are released into the community on **parole**. The TYC **Parole Program** was redesigned in 1998 and the new design includes:

- Increased accountability for youth returned to the community;
- Community service activities; and

- Enhanced public, private, state, and local services for youth and families.[20]

The Parole Program includes surveillance, resocialization, and sanctions. The program emphasizes juvenile participation in education, vocational training, employment, treatment, counseling, and community services. Juveniles are required to spend at least 40 hours per week in such constructive activities. There are three primary levels of parole supervision: intensive, moderate, and minimum. All juveniles begin the program on intensive supervision and move to less restrictive levels of supervision based on individual performance, including how well they comply with parole conditions and how well they meet individual case planning objectives.

To qualify for release from parole, a juvenile must be at the minimum level of parole supervision. Sanctions occur if juveniles violate parole program conditions or expectations. Parole Management involves identifying, gathering, and analyzing data on juvenile parole in Texas and compiling reports for program evaluation and review.

Juveniles who are granted parole must agree to a number of conditions of supervision. These include:

- must obey all federal, state, county, and city laws and ordinances
- must report any arrests or violations of the law (including minor citations) to his/her parole officer within five days
- may not change approved placement, leave the county of placement for more than 24 hours, or leave the state of Texas without the permission of his/her parole officer
- must notify his/her parole officer prior to any change of residence
- will not cause physical pain or bodily injury to any person (including him/herself)
- will not own, use, sell, or have in his/her control any deadly weapon, firearm, explosive devices, or ammunition
- will not use any controlled substance, alcohol, or intoxicant
- will submit to drug screening tests as instructed by his/her parole officer
- will not associate with anyone who is using or is in possession of a controlled substance, alcohol, intoxicant, drug paraphernalia, or weapon
- will not intentionally damage or destroy property
- will not associate with gang members or participate in gang activity
- will follow all instructions given by his/her parole officer and agree to meet all expectations outlined in the individual plan of supervision

All juveniles with determinate sentences and those classified as Violent A must remain in the parole program until reaching the age of 21. For other juveniles, successful completion of the parole program requires him/her to:

- meet his/her minimum length of stay
- meet all objectives of his/her individual case plan

- achieve three consecutive months (90 days) of 40-hour constructive activity weeks
- complete all required community service hours
- achieve the minimum level of surveillance
- achieve a designed success plan
- develop an effective and attainable discharge plan.[21]

NOTES

1. Texas Youth Commission - A Brief History of TYC (http://www.tyc.state.tx.us/about/history.html)
2. Texas Juvenile Probation Commission - The Texas Juvenile Justice System (http://www.tjpc.state.tx.us/about_us/juv_justice_overview.htm)
3. *Ibid*
4. *Ibid*
5. Texas Juvenile Probation Commission (2003). *The State of Juvenile Probation in Texas: Calendar Year 2002.* (http://www.tjpc.state.tx.us/publications/reports/RPTSTAT2002.pdf)
6. FC §54.01(e)
7. Texas Juvenile Probation Commission (2003). *The State of Juvenile Probation in Texas: Calendar Year 2002 op cit.*
8. Texas Juvenile Probation Commission - The Texas Juvenile Justice System, *op cit.*
9. Texas Juvenile Probation Commission (2003). *The State of Juvenile Probation in Texas: Calendar Year 2002 op cit.*
10. Texas Juvenile Probation Commission web site (http://www.tjpc.state.tx.us/default.htm)
11. Dallas County Probation services web site (http://www.dallascounty.org/html/citizen-serv/juvenile/probation/probationservices.htm
12. *Ibid*
13. *Ibid*
14. *Ibid*
15. Texas Youth Commission - Commitment Profile (http://www.tyc.state.tx.us/research/profile.html)
16. Texas Youth Commission - TYC Population Trends (http://www.tyc.state.tx.us/research/growth_charts.html)
17. *Ibid*
18. Texas Youth Commission - About TYC (http://www.tyc.state.tx.us/about/index.html)
19. *Ibid*
20. Texas Youth Commission - Parole Program Overview (http://www.tyc.state.tx.us/programs/parole1_overview.html)
21. *Ibid*

CHAPTER 10

DRUGS AND CRIME IN TEXAS

INTRODUCTION

Drug abuse is a serious problem in Texas, as in most states. A recent survey about substance abuse among adults in Texas found that almost 10 percent reported using an illicit substance during the previous year and almost 40 percent reported using an illicit substance at least once in their lives.[1] During 2001, the police in Texas made a total of 103,922 arrests for drug abuse violations. Of these, 9,650 (approximately 9 percent) were of juveniles. The majority of all drug arrests were for drug possession.[2] Illegal drugs enter the state from Mexico through a number of Texas cities, including El Paso, Laredo, and Brownsville, along with many smaller border towns; the drugs then move north for distribution through Houston and Dallas/Fort Worth. Drugs also move eastward from San Diego through Lubbock and from El Paso to Amarillo and Dallas/Fort Worth. Heroin and cocaine are imported into the country through Texas seaports and through the international airports in Houston and Dallas/Fort Worth.[3]

THE AVAILABILITY OF DRUGS IN TEXAS

Marijuana

According to the Drug Enforcement Administration, **marijuana** is readily available throughout the state and is the most widely-used illegal drug in Texas. Marijuana is imported into the state across the Mexican border, primarily in commercial trucks and privately owned vehicles. The U.S. Border Patrol routinely seizes extremely large quantities of the drug. At ports of entry, seizures of over a ton are not uncommon, while several hundred pounds may be taken from "backpackers" entering the country along the Rio Grande River. Marijuana is also grown and cultivated in the state, with indoor cultivation being a particular problem in North Texas.[4]

Marijuana was the primary problem for approximately 10 percent of all adults admitted to state-funded treatment programs in 2002. The average age of clients with marijuana problems has increased from 24 in 1985 to 27 in 2002. The proportion of juveniles admitted for marijuana abuse has increased from 35 percent in 1987 to 78 percent in 2001.[5]

Cocaine

Cocaine and **crack cocaine** are considered to be the most serious drug problem in Texas.[6] Crack cocaine is the primary illicit drug that is abused by adult clients who are admitted to publicly funded treatment programs in Texas. In 2001, 21 percent of all admissions were of crack cocaine users. In 2001, there were a total of 491 deaths in which cocaine was mentioned. This number has been increasing steadily since 1995. In 2001, the average age of individuals who died a cocaine-related death was almost 39 years. Of these, 42 percent were white, 28 percent were black, and 28 percent were Hispanic. Approximately 76 percent were male.[8]

The street costs of a rock of crack cocaine most commonly costs about $10, although prices may go as high as $100. The cost of a gram of powder cocaine varies by location. In Dallas, an ounce will cost between $50 and $80 while in Amarillo, Lubbock, and Alpine the price may reach $100. The price of powder cocaine tends to be cheaper nearer the Mexican border.[9]

Heroin

The most commonly used form of **heroin** in Texas is Mexican black tar. In Dallas, brown heroin is also becoming more easily available, as are Colombian and Southwest Asian heroin.[10] The cost of black tar heroin varies by location but street prices range from $10 to $20 per capsule or $500 to $4,500 per ounce. Mexican brown heroin costs $10 per capsule and $700 to $3,000 per ounce.[11]

Heroin is the third most commonly abused drug (after alcohol and crack cocaine) for which adult clients are admitted to state-funded substance abuse treatment programs. In 2002, 12 percent of all admissions were heroin users, up from 9 percent in 1993. Most addicts inject heroin, although a small percentage inhale the drug. The number of deaths that included a mention of heroin has decreased recently, from a high of 374 deaths in 1998 to 339 in 2001. The average age of individuals who died a heroin-related death in 2001 was 39.1 years. Of these, approximately 54 percent were white, 8 percent were black, and 36 percent were Hispanic. Approximately 81 percent were male.[12]

Methamphetamine

Methamphetamine is becoming increasingly available in parts of Texas, especially the Houston area. The two primary types found in the state are Mexican-manufactured methamphetamine, which is transported across the border in privately owned and commercial vehicles, and locally-produced methamphetamine, which is produced in small amounts in clandestine laboratories around the state.[13] The street price of Mexican methamphetamine is $400 per ounce or $5,800 to $9,000 per pound.[14]

Alcohol

Alcohol is the most commonly abused drug in Texas. In 2002, 35 percent of all adults admitted to publicly-funded treatment programs had a primary problem with alcohol use. The average age of these individuals was 38, higher than other substance abusers. Of these, 57 percent were white, 18 percent were black, and 23 percent were Hispanic. Approximately 71 percent were male. Alcohol use was the primary problem for 8 percent of all juveniles admitted for treatment. Of these, approximately 42 percent were white, 9 percent were black, and 47 percent were Hispanic. Approximately 66 percent were male.[15]

Drug Abuse among Juveniles

In 2002, the **Texas School Survey of Substance Abuse Among Students** surveyed over 53,000 students in grades seven through 12 regarding their use of tobacco, alcohol, inhalants, marijuana, cocaine, crack cocaine, hallucinogens, heroin, and other illicit drugs. The study found that 53 percent of students surveyed used some substance during the past school year while 74 percent reported some substance use during their lifetime. The most commonly-used substances were alcohol, tobacco, marijuana, inhalants, and Ecstacy. Overall, the study found that substance use has decreased in the last ten years.[16]

The lifetime use of tobacco appears to be decreasing. Lifetime use of tobacco had been approximately 55 percent since 1990 but dropped to 51 percent in the 2000 survey and 45 percent in 2002. The decrease was particularly significant among younger students. However, the study also found that cigarette smoking increased with grade level. Use of alcohol has also decreased since 1990, with 71 percent of students surveyed in 2002 reporting lifetime use and 35 percent reporting current use. Ecstacy use has increased significantly. In 2000, approximately 5 percent of students reported lifetime use of the drug, while in 2002, this figure increased to 9 percent. Overall, students attending schools near the Mexican border reported higher current and lifetime use of many drugs.[17]

According to the Texas Commission on Alcohol and Drug Abuse, approximately 68 percent of youths in TYC custody during Fiscal Year 2000 abused or were dependent on drugs or alcohol during the year before they entered a TYC facility.[18]

THE TEXAS COMMISSION ON ALCOHOL AND DRUG ABUSE

Originally, the Texas legislature separated the problems of alcohol and drug abuse by creating separate agencies to deal with each problem. In 1953, the legislature created the **Texas Commission on Alcoholism** (TCA). Although its original purpose was limited to distributing public information about alcoholism, the agency's responsibilities soon expanded and it became the primary authority on alcoholism for the state. In 1970, the governor created the **State Program on Drug Abuse**, which later became the **Drug Abuse Prevention Division** (DAPD) of the Texas Department of Community Affairs. DAPD was the state agency responsible for coordinating drug abuse programs and administering federal funds for drug abuse.

In 1985, the legislature merged the TCA and the DAPD to create the **Texas Commission on Alcohol and Drug Abuse** (TCADA). The purpose of the TCADA is to address serious substance abuse issues affecting Texas residents. The Commission is made up of six members who are appointed by the state governor with the advice and consent of the Senate. At least three of the members must have experience in activities such as business management, financial management, auditing, contract management, etc. Members of the TCADA serve staggered terms of six years.[19]

Section 461.001 of the Texas Health and Safety Code (HSC) outlines the basic policy of the TCADA:

> Chemical dependency is a preventable and treatable illness and public health problem affecting the general welfare and the economy of the state. The legislature recognizes the need for proper and sufficient facilities, programs, and procedures for prevention, intervention, treatment, and rehabilitation. It is the policy of this state that a chemically dependent person shall be offered a continuum of services that will enable the person to lead a normal life as a productive member of society.

The TCADA contracts with public and private agencies to provide services for the prevention and treatment of substance abuse in Texas. Currently, TCADA has contracts with over 200 community agencies, as well as licensing approximately 5,000 chemical dependency counselors and 820 treatment sites, and certifying programs for drug offenders, alcohol awareness for minors, and DWI education. Essentially, the TCADA provides for the delivery of services for substance abuse prevention, intervention, and treatment.[20]

The TCADA has established eleven **Prevention Resource Centers** throughout the state. Their function is to emphasize the importance of prevention through education; facilitate the dissemination of prevention information regarding alcohol, tobacco, and other drugs; and coordinate substance abuse prevention efforts.[21]

In FY 2002, the TCADA's operating budget was over $175 million. Prevention programs supported by the TCADA served 41,592 adults and 227,093 youth. In addition, intervention services funding by the Commission served 229,907 adults and 151,292 youth.[22]

TEXAS DRUG TREATMENT COURTS

Texas, like most other states, has developed treatment-based drug courts. A drug court is a special court which handles cases involving drug-addicted offenders through the use of extensive supervision and treatment. The court also increases the coordination of various agencies and resources available to drug abusers, increasing the cost-effectiveness of the programs, and providing the offender with access to a wide variety of programs and resources. The concept involves treating drug addicts in the criminal justice system, rather than placing them in prison or on probation. The first drug courts in Texas were established in 1993 in Travis and Jefferson Counties. It is two to three times more expensive to place an offender in a Texas drug court program than to place him or her on regular probation, but it is significantly less expensive than placing the offender in a secure prison facility.[22]

In 2001, the state passed legislation requiring all counties with populations of over 550,000 to create a drug court program. This appears to be in response to an increase in arrests and incarcerations for drug offenses. In 1990, there were 59,405 arrests for drug offenses; by 2000 this had increased by almost 63 percent to 96,646 arrests. During the same ten-year period, arrests for both violent and property offenses decreased. The number of offenders incarcerated in state jails and prisons for drug offenses increased from 8,988 to 33,477 between 1990 and 2000. While incarcerations for violent and property crimes also increased during this period, the increase was significantly less.[23]

Drug court programs in Texas range in length from 12 to 18 months. Most programs include requirements such as:

- offenders must attend weekly drug court hearings presided over by the drug court judge

- offenders must participate in counseling and treatment programs, and attend AA and/or NA meetings

- offenders must participate in regular drug testing

- offenders must meet regularly with case managers for progress reviews

Most programs also provide a variety of other services or referrals, including parenting classes, educational and vocational services, employment assistance, medical or mental health service referrals, and life skills training.

Offender participation in most drug court programs is voluntary. Offenders who meet program eligibility criteria may be offered drug court participation as an alternative to traditional criminal justice system processing. Eligibility criteria usually include:

- the offender was arrested for a drug-related offense (possession, prescription fraud, DWI)
- the offender was not involved in a violent offense
- the offender has a substance abuse problem and/or is chemically dependent[24]

The Travis County Drug Court

The **Travis County Drug Court** is known as the **SHORT** (the System of Healthy Options for Release and Transition) Court. The program, which is located in Austin, is administered by the Travis County Criminal Court. It is a diversion program for those offenders who meet the following criteria:

- arrested for felony-level possession of a controlled substance
- have no prior convictions for violent offenses
- have no other charges pending

SHORT is designed to provide opportunities for rehabilitation and is an alternative to traditional criminal processing. Participants waive their right to a trial and agree to obey the judge's orders, giving the judge more freedom in requiring them to go through counseling, in-patient drug treatment, etc.

The program lasts for approximately 15 months and includes heavy supervision, frequent drug screening (e.g., urinalysis), counseling (e.g., twelve-step meetings), family and parenting classes, school or job training, and participation in substance abuse treatment and education programs, and provides various support services for offenders. Each participant is assigned a primary counselor who assists him or her in completing the program. The SHORT judge is also active in developing case plans, providing treatment referrals, and handing down court sanctions. If a program participant tests negative for drugs and attends the requirement meetings and treatment programs for a prescribed period of time, the treatment plan will be modified by reducing the requirements (e.g., placing the offender on a lighter level of supervision).

If an offender successfully completes the SHORT program, remaining drug free for a court-specified period of time, the criminal charges will be dismissed. Offenders who resume using drugs or who fail to make adequate progress through the program may be moved back to a higher level of supervision; ordered to attend more counseling sessions or undergo more frequent drug testing; required to participate in a residential treatment program; or even be sent to jail for a period of time. Offenders who continue to abuse drugs may be returned to the court to face their original drug charge(s).[25]

The 243rd District Felony Drug Court Treatment Program

The **243rd District Felony Drug Court Treatment Program** is commonly known as the **El Paso Drug Court**. It focuses on non-violent felony drug offenders in an attempt to reduce recidivism among the treatment population. Participation in the program is limited to male and female offenders who meet the following criteria:

- must have a history of substance abuse
- must be at least 17 years of age
- must be a legal resident of El Paso County
- must have at least 24 months remaining on a sentence of probation
- must be capable of understanding and meeting the requirements of the program.

Certain categories of offenders are excluded from the program. These include:

- any offender with outstanding warrants or pending INS holds
- any violent offender with a criminal history of possession or use of a dangerous weapon
- any offender with a criminal history of crimes involving death or serious bodily injury, including sex offenses
- any offender on probation for possession or delivery of at least 200g of a controlled substance or at least 50lbs of marijuana
- any offender with at least 4 subsequent DWI convictions[26]

The program lasts approximately 18 months and includes three separate phases. **Phase I (Stabilization)** focuses on preparing the participant for drug treatment. Offenders in Phase I must adhere to the following requirements:

- make weekly appearances in Court and have frequent visits from a court surveillance team
- abstain from alcohol and other drugs
- regular attendance in AA and/or NA
- placement in a community-based treatment program
- develop an initial treatment plan with the Court, including drug treatment needs, education and vocational needs, and any other needs (healthcare, housing, etc.)
- participate in individual and group counseling sessions
- undergo regular drug testing
- report to a probation officer twice per week

To move out of Phase I and into Phase II, the participant must meet the following advancement requirements:

- complete at least four months in Phase I
- participate regularly in a community-based treatment program
- comply with all treatment plan goals and complete all prescribed objectives
- submit to drug testing as required
- have at least three consecutive months without Court sanctions
- acquire all necessary identification to begin meeting educational and vocational goals
- demonstrate an ability to keep all appointments with probation officer, drug court judge, treatment providers, etc.

Phase II (Maintenance) focuses on maintaining the goals developed in Phase I and on encouraging the participant to develop a lifestyle that involves abstaining from drugs and alcohol. Phase II requirements include:

- make biweekly appearances in Court and have frequent visits from a court surveillance team
- continue to abstain from alcohol and other drugs
- continue to participate in individual and group counseling sessions, and in AA/NA if appropriate
- review and update the initial treatment plan and goals
- continue to undergo regular drug testing
- participate in educational programs if applicable
- obtain employment or participate in a job training program
- report to a probation officer once each week

To advance to Phase II, the participant must:

- complete at least six months in Phase I
- complete all prescribed objectives
- have at least four consecutive months without Court sanctions
- demonstrate an ability to keep all appointments with probation officer, drug court judge, treatment providers, etc.
- successfully complete a community-based treatment program
- participate in an outside support system, such as AA or NA

The final part of the program, **Phase III (Transitioning)** focuses in preparing the participant for life outside the drug court program. To complete Phase III, and be released from the program, participants must meet the following requirements:

- make monthly appearances in Court and have frequent visits from a court surveillance team
- continue to abstain from alcohol and other drugs
- document weekly attendance in an outside support system (NA, AA, etc.)
- review and update program goals
- complete the GED or job training program if applicable
- show sustained employment for at least four months of this Phase
- report to a probation officer biweekly.[27]

NOTES

1. Wallisch, Lynn S. *2000 Texas Survey of Substance Use Among Adults.* Texas Commission on Alcohol and Drug Abuse. (http://www.tcada.state.tx.us/research/AdultHousehold.pdf)

2. Office of National Drug Control Policy (July, 2003). *State of Texas: Profile of Drug Indicators.* (http://www.whitehousedrugpolicy.gov/statelocal/tx/tx.pdf)
3. Gulf Coast Addiction Technology Transfer Center. *Substance Abuse Trends in Texas: June 2003.* (http://www.tcada.state.tx.us/research/trends/June2003.pdf)
4. DEA Fact Sheet: *Texas* (http://www.usdoj.gov/dea/pubs/states/texas.html)
5. Gulf Coast Addiction Technology Transfer Center. *Substance Abuse Trends in Texas: June 2003, op cit.*
6. Office of National Drug Control Policy (2003). *State of Texas: Profile of Drug Indicators.* (http://www.whitehousedrugpolicy.gov/statelocal/tx/tx.pdf)
7. DEA Fact Sheet: *Texas, op cit.*
8. Gulf Coast Addiction Technology Transfer Center. *Substance Abuse Trends in Texas: June 2003, op cit.*
9. *Ibid*
10. DEA Fact Sheet: *Texas, op cit.*
11. Office of National Drug Control Policy (2003). *State of Texas: Profile of Drug Indicators, op cit.*
12. Gulf Coast Addiction Technology Transfer Center. *Substance Abuse Trends in Texas: June 2003, op cit.*
13. DEA Fact Sheet: *Texas, op cit.*
14. Office of National Drug Control Policy (2003). *State of Texas: Profile of Drug Indicators, op cit.*
15. Gulf Coast Addiction Technology Transfer Center. *Substance Abuse Trends in Texas: June 2003, op cit.*
16. Liu, Llang Y. *Texas School Survey of Substance Abuse Among Students: Grades 7-12, 2002.* (http://www.tcada.state.tx.us/research/survey/grades7-12/SchoolSurvey2002.pdf)
17. *Ibid*
18. Wallisch, Lynn S. and Lisa Kerber (2001). *Substance Use and Delinquency Among Youths Entering Texas Youth Commission Facilities: 2000-2001.* Austin, TX: Texas Commission on Alcohol and Drug Abuse. (http://www.tcada.state.tx.us/research/youth_delinquency00-01.pdf)
19. Texas Commission on Alcohol and Drug Abuse web site (http://www.tcada.state.tx.us/)
20. *Ibid*
21. Texas Commission on Alcohol and Drug Abuse (2003). *2002 Annual Report.* (http://www.tcada.state.tx.us/policy_info/AnnualReport.pdf)
22. Criminal Justice Policy Council (January 2002). *Overview of Drug Courts in Texas.* Austin, TX: Criminal Justice Policy Council. (http://www.cjpc.state.tx.us/reports/parprob/drugcourt.pdf)
23. *Ibid*
24. *Ibid*
25. *Ibid*
26. 243rd District Felony Drug Court Treatment Program web site (http://www.co.el-paso.tx.us/wtc/drugcourt/default.htm)
27. *Ibid*

APPENDIX

WEB SITES OF INTEREST

There is a large amount of information on Texas and the Texas criminal justice system available on the World Wide Web. Below is a selection of web sites that may be of interest to students.

GENERAL TEXAS WEB SITES:

http://www.state.tx.us/

The State of Texas web site with information on Texas government, economy, education, health care, crime and much more. Links to a variety of state government agencies may be found on this site.

http://www.governor.state.tx.us/

The web site for the Office of the Governor of Texas.

http://www.capitol.state.tx.us/

The web site for the Texas Legislature, including links to the Senate, the House of Representatives, and a number of other state agencies.

http://www.oag.state.tx.us/

This is the web site for the Attorney General of Texas.

http://www.tsl.state.tx.us/

The web site of the Texas State Library and Archives Commission.

http://www.texasbar.com/public/consumerinfo/helpfulinfo/justice/process.asp

This link accesses a guide to the Texas criminal justice process, which has been prepared by the State Bar.

LEGAL INFORMATION ON TEXAS:

http://www.capitol.state.tx.us/txconst/toc.html

The Constitution of the State of Texas is available on the Internet.

http://www.capitol.state.tx.us/statutes/statutes.html

Texas state statutes are available on the World Wide Web. Statutes of interest include the Penal Code, the Code of Criminal Procedure, the Family Code, and the Government Code.

http://www.sos.state.tx.us/

The web site for the Texas Secretary of State includes a link to the Texas Administrative Code, which contains information on both public safety and corrections.

INFORMATION ON POLICE IN TEXAS:

http://www.txdps.state.tx.us/

The Texas Department of Public Safety web site.

http://www.ci.houston.tx.us/departme/police/home.htm

The web site of the Houston Police Department.

http://www.dallaspolice.net/

The web site of the Dallas Police Department.

http://co.jefferson.tx.us/sheriff/mission.htm

The Jefferson County Sheriff's Office web site.

http://www.co.harris.tx.us/so/

The Harris County Sheriff's Office web site.

http://www.tcleose.state.tx.us/

The web site of the Texas Commission on Law Enforcement Officer Standards and Education.

INFORMATION ON THE COURTS IN TEXAS:

http://www.courts.state.tx.us/

The web site for the Texas Judiciary. This page includes links to all the main types of courts in the state as well as many other court-related links.

http://www.courts.state.tx.us/oca/

The web site for the Texas Office of Court Administration.

http://www.weblocator.com/attorney/tx/search/index.html

The Attorney Locator for Texas includes a considerable amount of information on Texas Law. Some links of particular interest include: *Process of a Lawsuit*; *Criminal Law*; *Texas Court System*; and *Texas' Legal & Judicial System*.

http://www.texasbar.com/

The web site for the State Bar of Texas.

http://www.scjc.state.tx.us/index.php

The web site for the Texas State Commission on Judicial Conduct.

INFORMATION ON CORRECTIONS IN TEXAS:

http://www.tdcj.state.tx.us/index.htm

The web site of the Texas Department of Criminal Justice.

http://www.tdcj.state.tx.us/bpp/index.htm

The web site of the Texas Board of Pardons and Paroles.

http://www.tjcs.state.tx.us

The web site of the Texas Commission on Jail Standards.

http://www.tci.tdcj.state.tx.us/

The web site of Texas Correctional Industries.

http://www.tdcj.state.tx.us/stat/deathrow.htm

This web page provides statistics on the use of the death penalty in Texas.

http://www.tcadp.org/

This is the web site of the Texas Coalition to Abolish the Death Penalty.

INFORMATION ON THE TEXAS JUVENILE JUSTICE SYSTEM:

http://www.tyc.state.tx.us/index.html

The web site of the Texas Youth Commission.

http://www.tjpc.state.tx.us/

The Texas Juvenile Probation Commission web site.

http://www.dhs.state.tx.us/

The web site of the Texas Department of Human Services.

http://www.dallascounty.org/html/citizen-serv/juvenile/probation/probationservices.htm

The web site of the Dallas County Juvenile Department

INFORMATION ON DRUGS IN TEXAS:

http://www.tcada.state.tx.us/

The Texas Commission on Alcohol and Drug Abuse web site.

http://www.whitehousedrugpolicy.gov/statelocal/tx/tx.pdf

The Office of National Drug Control Policy provides a large amount of information on drug use statistics and drug prevention efforts in Texas.

http://www.usdoj.gov/dea/pubs/states/texas.html

A DEA fact sheet on drug in Texas.

http://www.co.el-paso.tx.us/wtc/drugcourt/default.htm

The web site for the 243rd District Felony Drug Court Treatment Program